The Ultimate Wedding Reception

Volume 1

Mark G. Imperial

Published by
Game Changers Multimedia
1415 W. 22nd St. Tower Floor
Oak Brook, IL 60523
Phone: 1-877-349-2615

Printed in the United States of America

ISBN-13: 978-0985887513
ISBN-10: 0985887516

This book is dedicated to every Bride and Groom.
May your wedding day be filled with Happiness, Excitement,
and Lasting Memories.

Table of Contents

Part I

11   Mark G. Imperial's Story

13   How to Get the Most Out of This Book

17   Your First Party as Husband and Wife

23   Your DJ Entertainer as Master of Ceremonies
Can Be Both The Coordinator and The Voice

31   Dissection of an Amazing Celebration
by an Entertainment and Music Programmer

39   Insider Secrets to Your Reception's Music
Programming from a Music Programmer

47   Seven Essential Truths About DJ Entertainers

69   Your DJ Entertainer Hiring Checklist

71   How to Make Sure Your DJ Rocks the House

79   Can I DJ My Own Wedding Reception
Using an iPod?

Part II

89   You Don't Need a DJ, You Need a Superhero!
     Mark Brenneisen, CSGI Events

101 Why a Top-Notch DJ Does Not
     Specialize in Music
     Guy Artis, OHS Entertainment

109 Give Your Reception the Winning Edge
     Raymond Williams, Ebony Connections

119 Get Your Money's Worth,
     Or Get Your Money Back!
     Kenya Conway, 2Fyne Entertainment

129 The Practice of Perfect Planning
     Jimmie Esposito, Move It Music DJ and Lighting

143 How to Have a Stress-free Event!
     Javier Montes, Entertainment Management Group

153 Getting More from Your DJ
     *Dr. Don Galbo, The Music Revue DJ's,
     Sound and Lighting Productions*

163 A Moral Obligation
     *Steve "Champagne" Sala,
     A Shining Star Production*

171   Raising the Bar for Your Day
       Barry Reynolds, DJ Wizard Entertainment

179   The Ingredients for Awesome
       Entertainment at Your Wedding
       *Chad Day, Have A Nice Day Mobile
       Entertainment*

187   Shhh! There's No Secret to Being a DJ
       Mike Gintella, Mike's Light and Sound

197   Don't Sabotage Your Own Wedding
       Dave Petry, DJ Dave Productions

209   Surviving Wedding Worst-Case
       Scenarios Like a Champ!
       *Mari Odette-Kanotz,
       A Amorè Events and Entertainment*

217   To Plan, Anticipate, Celebrate, and Remember
       Nick Javier, It's Time Entertainment

227   Keeping You Out of the Danger Zone
       *Robert & Stephanie Poff,
       Station Identification Entertainment*

241   What Matters Most—Experience You Can Trust
       *Tim MacMillan,
       MacMillan Entertainment Group*

247   How Do You Know if You Hired a Great DJ?
Austin Giles, Outright Entertainment

257   Making Your Reception a Memory,
Not Just an Event!
Gerald Chmilar, Prairie Mobile Music

269   Final Words and Advice
Mark Imperial

Part I

The Ultimate Wedding Reception

Mark G. Imperial's Story

Since dressing up as a member of Kiss with full makeup as a kid, Mark G. Imperial has been addicted to making people dance, sing, laugh, and smile. Being a breakdancer, "Karate Kid," and bedroom DJ through middle school and high school got him picked-on in school.

Mark learned to channel his inner-performer-nerd, as an entertainer and party host, founding his first DJ Entertainer business before the age of 21. Mark's passion for "everything party" expanded from just *playing* the music to actually forming his own record label and *making* the music that has hit dance music and club charts worldwide.

It was when Mark was the DJ for the late Walter Payton's nightclub chain that he discovered the art of **bringing out the best of**

each party by allowing the guests to be the stars. Mark and his team of certified DJ Entertainers brought his finely tuned talents to the wedding world, and couples flocked to his revolutionary style of entertainment as a catalyst of energy, letting the party guests shine.

Some of the world's most famous brands, including Nintendo and UnderArmour, discovered Mr. Imperial and his team's style, and frequently retain them for corporate celebrations, sales events, and product launches.

Don't call him a "guru." Although Mark is a thought-leader and top trainer in the DJ Entertainer industry, with more than 3,500 DJ students training under him worldwide. He brings his business knowledge to the airwaves as one of the hosts of Game Changers Radio Show on Chicago's Intelligent Talk WIND radio.

Mark attributes his being able to thrive under immense pressure to his years as a relief pitcher starting in Little League, being put in the game with bases loaded and zero outs. Outside of party-time, Mark is an avid kickboxer, which explains why he knows the virtues of mastering skills. He lives in the west suburbs of Chicago with his girlfriend Christina, a Pug named Otis, and a French Bulldog named Sadie. Mark will never turn down Thai, Vietnamese, or Mediterranean food.

Mark Imperial
888–523–1987
mark@markimperial.com
www.markimperial.com

Foreword

How to Get the Most Out of This Book

What I loved most about growing up in the Midwest, Chicagoland to be specific, was the incredible diversity in DJ entertainment. Chicago is known as one of the greatest epicenters for DJ Entertainers, so it was incredibly competitive, inspirational, and a heck of an incredible ride to launch a DJ career here. To succeed here, to rise above the competition, and to be recognized and hired by some of the world's most famous brands amidst very worthy competitors really means a lot. What I loved most about growing up in the Midwest, Chicagoland to be specific, was the incredible diversity in DJ entertainment. Chicago is known as one of the greatest epicenters for DJ Entertainers, so it was incredibly competitive, inspirational, and a heck of an incredible ride to launch a DJ career here. To succeed here, to rise above the competition, and to be recognized and hired by some of the world's most famous brands amidst very worthy competitors really means a lot.

This is the book that I wished I had and had available for my clients over the years. I've taken years of my behind-the-scenes experience to create this tell-all book to show you what it really looks like to create a terrific wedding reception. This book is not meant to be biased in any way, but to simply report the facts and let you decide what is important.

I will cover many aspects of the wedding reception. This is not meant to be just from the entertainment's perspective, although you will find where the entertainment fits as a catalyst for your celebration.

There are many books, websites, and wedding magazines that choose to cover every aspect of the wedding from A to Z. I chose to go deep on one subject, which is the wedding reception, where I feel the information is lacking.

This Book Is Like Having 2 Books in 1

In part one, I am happy to share the behind-the-scenes ingredients that go into a great reception. These won't just be the common things you will read in generalist books. Instead, you'll discover little-known secrets, facts, and unspoken truths.

You may also be shocked when I reveal to you the "dark side" of the DJ Entertainer industry, which, quite frankly, some of the worst offenders hope you never hear. Over the years, I've heard so many wedding vendors complain about some of the things I will reveal, but until now no one's had the guts to tell.

The good news is that I'll give you tons of great tips and things to look for and keep in mind while you plan your big day's celebration finale. I'll walk you past the big landmines, make you aware of some of the gotchas so you can avoid them, and keep you focused for success.

You'll get the seven essential truths about DJ Entertainers, including a hiring checklist. And once you hire your DJ Entertainer, I'll share with you the biggest things to focus on so you can get the best performance of their career for YOUR reception!

Mark dancing with M&M Mars Candy founding family.

In part two, I'll introduce to you 18 of the world's leading DJ Entertainers. I have personally invited them to contribute tips, tricks, and secrets coming from their experiences in their part of the world. These DJ Entertainers have been invited because they have demonstrated their passion and commitment to serving their clients.

You should look to these DJ Entertainer chapters for big ideas, inspirations, and themes. Some will share different, unexpected challenges they faced, and how they overcame them by thinking on their feet.

You'll find part two to be a refreshing way to round out the knowledge base of this book. Before this one, there has never been a book created that shares as many ideas and perspectives from top professionals for your benefit.

Enjoy this book, and have a great time!

Chapter One

Your First Party as Husband and Wife

If you have a great family and a great set of friends, you are already set for a great reception. The rest of the details of your reception are either going to enhance your celebration, be neutral, or degrade the experience—this is where we will explore ways to be sure you have the big day of your dreams.

The purpose of this book is to give you an unbiased, fact-based view of what makes a wedding reception unforgettable and successful. We will view all the little-known or rarely considered truths that every bride and groom should know.

Your First Big Bash as Husband and Wife

This book has been crafted to help you create **Your Ultimate Wedding Reception**, which essentially will be the first party for family and friends that you throw as husband and wife. It is designed to show you behind the wizard's curtain, so you can gain a better perspective of what propels your party. There are plenty of books on the subject of weddings, many which cover the A to Z of wedding planning. This is NOT one of those books. In this book, I've intentionally chosen to focus on the wedding reception because it is so often misunderstood and contains the most moving parts. With your big day comes many details that must be attended to, but the one unshakeable truth, whether we like it or not, whether we agree or not, is that the success of all your hard work and planning will hinge on your reception.

When Your Family and Friends Get Together, Your Reception Is Already Set for Success... The Right Match of Vendors Can Bring Out the Very Best

Your ceremony is technically the main event, but it's your reception that will be the icing on the cake, where everyone will celebrate with you. It makes sense because it is the most social part of the entire experience. You're there to celebrate, loosen the tie, enjoy a glass of champagne, and cut loose!

Although every detail of your wedding planning is important, survey after survey of brides post-wedding reveals that nearly 100%, in hindsight, would have given their reception entertainment

Did you know George Foreman has DJ kids?

choice a higher priority.

This book will give you the information you need to assure your wedding reception is successful. Having been involved in hundreds of wedding reception planning sessions with brides and grooms, and having performed as Master of Ceremonies for them, I will give you my best observations from the front lines. I've also invited 18 top DJ Entertainers to contribute their first-hand experiences in creating unforgettable events across the United States and Canada.

The main objective of this book is to give you the most comprehensive information about running a successful wedding reception from the perspective of the people who direct them for you—your DJ Entertainer, who often serves as Master of Ceremonies.

First, let's take a look at why this is so important...

The Overall Success of Your Reception Hinges On You Having the Right Master of Ceremonies

An easily overlooked requirement for a successful wedding reception, or any party, for that matter, is someone who will be responsible for keeping everyone on schedule. Without someone in this role, it can be a very unpleasant experience and lead to a lot of awkward moments for your guests. This is typically the job of your Master of Ceremonies, and the tool that your Master of Ceremonies will use is a microphone.

Earlier I mentioned that a DJ Entertainer often serves as Master of Ceremonies, "MC" for short. For now, let's look at the MC's role in general.

In some cases, there may be situations where you won't have music or a microphone, and we'll talk about that in a minute. The majority of receptions will involve entertainment of some sort and will need someone to act as director.

Ideally, there would be a planner or coordinator who creates the agenda or timeline. All of the formalities, the food, the traditions, and the dancing would all be laid out on the timeline. That coordinator would be responsible for managing a punch list and making sure that every vendor is in the right place at the right time for every detail on that timeline. This is similar to the job of a project manager.

Then, someone would be the "voice" of your reception, making all of the important announcements and the introductions of the wedding party; announcing the formalities, traditions, and special dances in order to spotlight them; and generally giving a sense of comfort to your guests that everything is well organized.

Then, for the reception's entertainment portion, if you are having entertainment or dancing, that same voice would provide the energy and the mood for the celebration. Something I learned from my years working for the late Walter Payton's Entertainment One company was that the guests always feel the energy coming from the person on the microphone, which was always the DJ Entertainer at his events and properties.

Walter's company was very successful because they quickly identified that the success of their parties, and how long people stayed and enjoyed themselves, was a direct result of how well their DJ Entertainers performed. Also, the DJ Entertainers energy level was affected by their mood, so the company always made sure their DJs were the happiest people in the company! You might be surprised to know that it wasn't about the money; our DJs really just wanted a little bit of appreciation for what they did passionately. I personally remember DJs in bad moods killing the energy, ending the night early, and therefore killing the sales. On the other hand, I remember being part of record-setting nights when I and my other DJ colleagues were in the greatest mood ever. It showed with perfect musical sets and incredibly timed "left turns" that kept the dancing crowd on their toes, always excited with anticipation to hear what may be coming next!

Chapter Two

Your DJ Entertainer as Master of Ceremonies Can Be Both The Coordinator and The Voice

The most successful receptions and events I've attended, or been involved with, have utilized the DJ Entertainer in a dual role of Coordinator and Voice. The more descriptive term we will use is "Master of Ceremonies" or MC. Your MC will be responsible for the flow of the entire event, beyond the music and entertainment. Some folks in our industry refer to the DJ Entertainer as the Entertainment Director, but I feel that title doesn't encompass the entire role they play.

A reception without any Master of Ceremonies is like a circus without a ringmaster. As you might imagine, without leadership, there would be animals—lions, tigers, bears, and dogs—running amok!

Mark and crew with Shigeru Miyamota, Godfather of Nintendo, in New York City.

Imagine an airport without air traffic control! Lives would be at risk!

Fortunately, at your reception, lives wouldn't be at stake, but I'd imagine you wouldn't want to "Evacuate the Dance Floor" or have "No Parking on the Dance Floor" yuk-yuk.

The reason that the DJ Entertainer as Master of Ceremonies works best is because they set the mood and best understand the flow of the event. Have you ever seen the movie Office Space, when they asked Richard Reile's character to justify his role as liaison between the customer support people and the technical support people? His response was that the two departments couldn't talk to each other without mayhem, and he somehow acts as translator.

Hilarious, but that reminds me of what we are talking about here.

I think a wedding planner who really knows his or her stuff has spent a lot of time consulting with a DJ Entertainer, or was one, because of the amount of understanding you need to have to keep an event flowing smoothly. I've seen many zealous wedding planners foul up a moment by forcing something to happen when it shouldn't. Nothing clears a dance floor (and the mood) worse than bad timing! What an experienced DJ Entertainer knows best is timing.

Your Banquet Manager Needs a DJ Entertainer Who Is a Team Player and Doesn't Have an Ego

Over the years, I've really come to respect the job of the banquet manager and coordinator. Many are very tough, but they have to be in order to run a tight ship. To simultaneously serve hundreds of people a great dinner involves the coordination of dozens of people and resources—that is no simple feat! They need a DJ Entertainer who will respect their needs and not just ignore them to push their own agenda.

Without naming names, I've seen many DJ Entertainers butt heads unnecessarily with banquet managers. I hear these DJs rant about how they know how to throw a party better than a caterer, and instead of offering solutions, they prefer to deliberately sabotage a caterer or the banquet manager's duties. This is obviously an ego play, serves no one well, and ends of reducing the experience rather than enhancing it. I suppose, to some folks, performing as a DJ Entertainer can get to their head and they feel the need to entertain themselves by making others look bad. Personally, my reward comes from the greatest success of the event, and seeing a couple's big day play out beyond their wildest dreams.

It's easy to understand why many DJ Entertainers don't get along with catering managers, but it's unnecessary and foolish to not work together. The caterer has a job to do, and a product and service they need to deliver efficiently for the best experience of the guests. Sometimes their objectives may not flow well with the entertainment needs of the reception. A professional and mature DJ Entertainer will recognize that they should work together with the coordinator and offer solutions, not criticisms. The show flow can be flawless when the coordinator and your DJ Entertainer work closely together. When they are on the same team, the DJ Entertainer can accomplish their mission, which is to . . .

Bring Out the Very Best Feelings, Mood, and Energy from the Celebration Using Entertainment, Timing, Delivery, and Music

Notice that I actually put the word "music" last. One big misconception in our industry is that your DJ simply provides music. Many bridal websites and magazines proliferate this misinformation, but it's not their fault.

If you only look at it on the surface, you think "DJ" = "music," that must make sense? We've grown up thinking of the DJ on the radio introducing and playing music. Then it gets even funnier...when the celebration is ultra successful and the party goes off without a hitch, it means that the DJ Entertainer's extra preparation time, planning, and delivery paid off. What this means is their hard work and hours of preparation to create seamlessness and invisibility should go unnoticed! On the surface, it just looks like music! If the introductions, segues, or announcements are awkward, that's when you notice the lack of preparation.

Let's Suppose You're Not Having Entertainment, Let's Look at the Possibilities

If you're planning a very casual reception that won't involve music or entertainment, you may not need an official Master of Ceremonies, but you will need a way to direct the activities. Even if you won't have a microphone, you'll still want to consider who will be calling the shots and directing your formalities. Without a microphone, they'll probably have to go table to table to make their announcements. This can be the job of your wedding planner, if you are using one. If this will be another person or a member of the wedding party, you'll want to make extra sure that they are the right person for this position. They have strong leadership and communication skills, as they will be interfacing with not just your guests, but with your professional vendors.

Who Will You Appoint for This Big Role?

There are many elements that you must take into consideration when deciding who can help you in the role of Master of Ceremonies. Keep in mind that everyone means well, and many of your family or friends will want to help. Here are some things to keep in mind…

This will test your relationship with this person, so don't take it lightly. Planning your wedding reception is a really big commitment. Will you have one person helping you with everything from

A-Z? Or will you have one person only helping you manage your vendors, and another person focusing entirely on running the reception? A person just helping you run the reception is typically known as a "day of" consultant.

Will this person take the role seriously? Where does their experience come from? Has the person you are considering been involved in planning their own wedding? If so, they may already know that it's serious business. Don't choose someone who may bail on you for any reason—there's a lot at stake, including a bunch of your money. A running theme you should keep in mind is that there are no do-overs!

There are hundreds of tiny details that your Master of Ceremonies must consider. For example, before any planned activity or formality, they must remember to coordinate with your photographer and videographer first! Many once-in-a-lifetime memories and moments have been lost forever simply because no one thought of the photographer, and they may have been capturing something else or in the bathroom! You can't un-slice the cake, and re-staging your father/daughter dance will ruin the moment. Does your prospective Master of Ceremonies have the experience to know about all the things that happen behind-the-scenes of a wedding reception?

If you'd prefer not to impose on a family member or friend for this role, you could turn to a "day-of" consultant, or at minimum, enlist the help of your coordinator from the venue. However, be forewarned that the venue coordinator has a lot of other responsibilities in the back of the house that may interfere with their ability to give you the attention you need.

A professional "day-of" consultant typically takes all of your agenda information and makes sure your vendors are where they need to be at all times during your reception. They are able to give you the full time attention you need because they can focus on managing the main players, and not managing staff. One thing I can tell you from experience is that it is difficult to be in the moment and enjoy your once-in-a-lifetime wedding reception if you manage your own show. Instead of creating memories of magical moments, you'll be mired in checklists, become a wrangler of vendors, a puppet-master of staff, as you end up working when you should be celebrating.

Even if you don't plan on having music or entertainment, you may be able to enlist Master of Ceremonies service from a DJ Entertainer. Their experience can give you invaluable help with your timeline and objectives.

Chapter Three

Dissection of an Amazing Celebration by an Entertainment and Music Programmer

I've spent a decade of my life studying and perfecting entertainment and music programming for the late Walter Payton's company, Entertainment One. I was in charge of the auditioning and training of new DJ Entertainers for a number of their nightclub properties, along with creating the entertainment and music format for each club. Before working for Entertainment One, I had worked at a number of nightclubs but had never before seen the amount of innovation and research into the actual "entertainment as profit center" that Walter's company dedicated to the business. This may seem obvious as I explain it now, but even to this day, many bar and nightclub owners spend more of their time thinking that their deliverables stop at their food, decor (theme), and customer service. Often, these businesses think of their entertainment or DJ as an "oh, by the way," rather than a priority. At Entertainment One, our philosophy was that the DJ Entertainer (senior programmer, the title I held) was going to be the happiest person in the company because they directly affected the growth of sales and popularity for the properties. In the land of the party, the man with the plan, the engaging style, the microphone, and the music was king!

The Sweet Science of Entertainment Programming

Entertainment and music programming is a sweet science that is seldom talked about and even less understood. Over the decade, we experimented with music formats and tracked guest behavior, quality of guest experience, and sales on an hourly basis. Each hour, we could tell you which dance sets packed the dance floor and what caused thirsty guests to spike sales. We knew things that drove profits and popularity that other nightclubs deemed unimportant! Before working there, I enjoyed being a DJ Entertainer...but after working there, I LOVED being a DJ Entertainer! Everything I learned there is what I've found to be the ultimate formula for a successful event that involve entertainment, and that is what I will share with you in this chapter.

First, let's take a look at themes or style, in the context of how they can affect the success of your reception.

Theme Events and Style

In the nightclub business, we have a different philosophy about "themes" so you understand the context and the difference from clubs to your party. Our philosophy was similar to that of "build it and they will come." We would profile the demographic we wanted to serve and create an attraction that would be irresistible to them. In our area, many nightclubs were the same—they offered the dance floor, fancy lights, great sound system, and the exact same copycat, rubberstamp-like DJ playing what they heard at every other night-club. From this dilemma was born an opportunity—Entertainment One asked themselves, "How can we create an environment that is immersive, engaging, yet completely unexpected so that we garner maximum attention and connect at a deeper level with our guests?"

What they came up with was utterly bizarre, yet hugely success-ful! The new restaurant nightclub was to be called The Big Kahuna. On the surface, it appeared to be a beach club theme, complete with giant wave-wall, stuffed sharks, tiki huts lined with fruit lights, and a giant Betty Boop in a hula skirt. Fun stuff, but what's the big deal? What we did musically was as uncommon as a one-legged golfer!

While every other nightclub in the Chicago suburbs played the same club music (some people still call it disco) and R&B, we decid-ed to cater to the rest of the population who were underserved—in our area, that was the new wave, alternative, pop, and underground crowds! It's hard to believe, but as popular as groups like Depeche Mode, The Cure, INXS, and Duran Duran were in that day, you'd rarely hear them in the nightclubs!

It was quite bizarre. You would walk into a beach club, expect to hear either fifties or sixties beach music or typical disco-fare, but instead you'd hear Nine Inch Nails "Head Like a Hole" or Ministry "Halloween." Now, the shock to the system of the consumer caused some push back, of course, but a smart club owner will stay the

Mark with Ivanka Trump in Chicago

course and carve out their uniqueness, while others would cave and before you know it, they're just another copycat bar with no reason to exist in a sea of sameness. Big Kahuna stayed its course and created company record-breaking $120K weeks in sales with lines wrapped around the building every weekend.

Using "Themes" in Your Reception

Now, the difference I want to point out to you is that with a nightclub, we chose the "who" we WANTED and reverse engineered how we would get them. In the case of YOUR wedding reception, you already KNOW who you are inviting, so you can super-engineer your reception to make them happy!

I've seen themes executed well that the guests will never forget, and other themes that the hosts wish people would forget! I have one simple, mega-important tip for you if you wish to use a theme for your reception—and that is to "play" on your theme, but don't make it the entire event. I'll give you an example...

I helped a couple create an event where the guests of honor were huge fans of arena rock music—you know, the "big hair" kind of music. Well, yes, it's party music, but that depends on whom you ask.

Originally, they envisioned everything about the reception having to do with that popular era of music. Naturally, they thought that the entire playlist should only consist of that music.

Early in my career, I didn't think much about this, and I always felt that the client is always right. I always gave the client the benefit of the doubt. That is, until I saw a theme completely blow up, where we had to come to the rescue (more about this in a minute). An experienced DJ Entertainer should always listen to your requests but be able to ask you clarifying questions to be sure you're both on the same page, and that you understand what you're requesting.

Upon further planning with the arena rock client, we discovered that although this couple and a handful of friends were gung ho about big hair music, they realized that their family and the majority of guests might not agree.

We adjusted the plan so that they could have a completely personalized arena rock–style reception from the invitations to the decor. We even created a special medley mini-dance set using their favorite retro rock hits, but we used them as peak hour left turns and highlights rather than letting them fizzle.

During formalities, transitions, and times where we needed low background music, we would again use arena rock song selections to keep the feeling going.

The big lesson here is that you retain the variety of music choices that all of your guests will enjoy, while infusing enough of your theme music and theme songs where they can be most effective in setting the atmosphere.

The Night When Country Line-Dancing Went *Off*-line

Now, about the theme that flew like a lead balloon…

There is a reason we became more selective about the clients we work with. No job is worth any amount of revenue if you can't assure the success of the reception—either because you're not a good match for them, or the couple has demands that you know will be challenging and they are unwilling to hear your suggestions even when they come from a place of experience.

Many years ago, when I needed the business and would accept any job I could get, I accepted a wedding reception for a couple that were huge country music line dancing fans. My gut told me it would be a huge problem, but I told myself I'd get through it.

The couple insisted on having nothing but country music line dancing at the reception. I did my best to point out possible pushback from their guests, but they insisted that it was "their day" and to heck with what anybody else thought. I even made them reflect on who they were actually inviting. That should have been my big red flag to get out of Dodge, but I needed the business. I asked them a very direct question: "When you go out country line dancing, are all of your friends and family (everyone you're inviting) there loving it, too?" I even went as far as to hire a specialist in leading country line dancing for the night, a person I've known from working the corporate event market.

We were totally prepared to deliver the most kick-butt country music line dancing party ever! Only three songs into the dancing portion of the night, a mob formed with torches (at least it felt that way), surrounding the DJ booth, asking, "Is this all we are going to hear all night?" Uh, oh. Not good.

Keeping to my promise and not to make the couple appear at fault (read: I took one for the team), I said, "Yes, this is the format for the evening." Oh boy, did I get grief. After having guest after guest approach me with the same question, and after absorbing brutal criticism and insults, I decided I would never take a job that I didn't believe in or that would cause me to be inauthentic. I would never pass the blame to a couple, so we kept with the plan, but I did point out that people were asking.

Without my suggestion, their guests must've bugged them enough and shown enough disinterest on the dance floor, because the bride approached us at the DJ booth to say, "Play whatever they want to hear, do whatever you need to do to get this party rocking." Music to my ears. We then adjusted the game plan, put our music programming hats back on, and rocked the house. On-the-fly, as I suggested earlier, we infused country music during transitions, slow sets, a mini-line dance set, and where it was appropriate to keep the feeling of their theme.

Fortunately, the night turned out to be a huge success, and

the line dancing was actually appreciated in proper doses. It also taught me to trust my gut more.

I hope these two examples help illustrate the dos and don'ts of using a theme for your reception.

Chapter Four

Insider Secrets to Your Reception's Music Programming from a Music Programmer

L et me tell you about an epic fail of mine so you can avoid the same landmine. When I first started to DJ, long before I ever attempted to entertain at a wedding reception (thankfully), I had a completely different impression of what it would take to be a DJ. In my mind, I thought that if I knew music well, and was familiar with the most popular songs on the radio and in the nightclubs, there just wasn't any way I could miss. Also in my mind, I saw myself as a party rocker and chick magnet! That all left my mind one fateful night, a night I had rehearsed and planned for months. I thought I was thoroughly prepared, and boy, I was wrong.

After being a bedroom DJ for so many months, a friend actually asked me to play at a party he was having at the neighborhood clubhouse. Boy, was I excited! All the months of party rocking to my dog in my bedroom was going to pay off.

I listened to the radio for weeks and jotted down all the top songs. I took note of every request that was phoned into the station. It's funny to think now, that before the Internet, you had to look pretty hard to find a radio top 40 list!

In my bedroom, I wrote down the playlist including all the top 40 songs almost in order. I practiced my "mix" in front of a mirror and just imagined a packed dance floor screaming for more. I was ready!

When I got to the party, it was like high comedy, with disasters one after the other. First, I had my headphones on my head and the plug was in my pocket because I had forgotten to plug it into the mixer. I was panicking because the last DJ's song was ending, and I thought there was a problem with the mixer because I couldn't hear my first record I put on in my headphones because they weren't plugged in! Then the worst thing in the world...dead air! I had to start the song from the very beginning because I couldn't hear it to cue it properly.

Another DJ showed me that I had not plugged my headphones in and that the plug was in my pocket. Wow, that was embarrassing! Fortunately, he was a nice guy and didn't tell anyone else what a bonehead I was.

The next problem, I had put on one of the top three songs on the charts at that time, but only two people danced. In a bit of a panic, I threw on the number one song and didn't get any more response at all! What was happening here? The rest of my set was pretty much flat. The most people I got on the floor was at the end, when I put on a slow song before the next DJ. My heart sunk. Why was it that I could have all of the most popular songs, yet not be able to get anyone to dance? I figured out the answer to that question when I heard the next DJ, who was a veteran with tons of experience with real people dancing on his dance floor.

The DJ that followed me didn't start with a top song at all. What I learned later was that he actually started with what we call a "recurrent" hit. His first few songs got a huge response that built up the dance floor. He had them whipped up into a total frenzy. People were having a blast dancing and even singing along. At certain parts of the song, he would lower the volume and the crowd would sing the lyrics louder, it was amazing! I was taking a lot of mental notes as I realized I could learn a lot from this experience.

What the DJ did next blew my mind. Somehow, he knew that the crowd couldn't keep up that pace without burning out. So when the time was right, he hit them with his peak song, then followed up with something completely different! As I was taking notes, I called that a "left turn," which I still refer to as today. The crowd ate it up; he had them completely under his spell, and they didn't grow tired.

The biggest take away for me that night was **_learning that it didn't matter if I had all the most popular songs in the world if I didn't know when and how to play them!_** That was my first exposure to real-life music programming, and this guy was the king! Of course, I swallowed my pride and asked if I could hang around and learn more from him. Thankfully, he said, "Sure, a lot of these guys just don't understand the art, and they certainly don't appreciate the skill." He went on to tell me something that sticks with me to this day: "A lot of people think that DJs are failed musicians, but the truth is our craft is blending their songs (their art) together in

Mark Imperial certified entertainment team.

a way that make people dance—and it takes a heck of a lot of talent to know just how to do that."

The Craft of Music Programming:
Say NO to the "Human Jukebox"

After discovering that just having the music wasn't enough, and that the DJ needs experience in music programming, my world was turned upside down. What I thought was an easy job where I can just play my favorite tunes turned out to be actual work. Don't get me wrong, it was work I wanted to do, but it wasn't going to be easy, at least at first.

As I followed my DJ mentor, I learned many things to do, and hundreds of things not to do. I'll share with you just the key takeaways. For the purpose of this book, I will clarify how each point relates directly to your reception.

For one, know your audience, including their tastes and age ranges. Your DJ should want to learn as much as possible about your guests. He or she will prepare as much as possible before hand tailoring their style to your audience. The only exception is if you are hiring talent specifically for their own unique style, similar to why you would see a particular band, but this is relatively rare.

Once your DJ knows your audience, they will still have a handful of popular but specific selections that they will throw out as little "tests" to learn your audience's tastes by their reactions. The most experienced programmers can learn your audience within a few songs. This is a high-level skill that only comes with experience, and is rarely understood by new or inexperienced DJs.

The Skillfully Crafted "Left Turn"

Two, no matter how great the dance set is going, your DJ must know when to do a left turn so as not to let the set go too long. Letting the dance floor dwindle and die on its own is not what you should go for. An awesome music programmer thinks in terms of ending sets on high notes, which leaves dancers wanting more. This is what keeps people excited and engaged all night, rather than looking at their watches!

The left turn is not meant to kill a dance floor, but rather create energy by introducing another popular style of music that is just as fun, but just different. A good left turn will actually also turn your dance floor. Some folks will stay, some will grab a drink at the bar, and some folks who were sitting will jump on the floor! The whole idea behind the left turn is making sure there is never too long of a period where someone hasn't heard something they like.

The whole concept of music programming is so vitally important for wedding receptions because they are so often attended by such a wide range of music fans. You can't please everyone with one style of music, you have to have a plan!

The Right Songs and the Right Versions

Three, be sure that you see eye to eye with your DJ Entertainer about your songs and the versions you'd like to hear because there is a difference.

This is especially important when working for families that will have young children in the audience. Don't assume playing appropriate music will go without saying. Be sure that your DJ Entertainer will only play radio clean versions of songs. Just because a song is considered "radio clean" doesn't mean that it won't have inappropriate lyrics, so have a discussion about your feelings on that.

The Request Line

Four, have a great understanding with your DJ Entertainer about handling requests. In my experience, it's best to have four columns on your request list:

1. Must Play Songs
2. Please Play Songs
3. Only If They Beg Songs
4. Never Play Songs

In a later chapter titled "How to Get the Best Performance from Your DJ Entertainer," I'll go into more detail about how to craft the best playlist or request list, but for now, I'll give you an overview. The way I see it is that the client is mostly right, but should be open to suggestions if they miss out on something that will really enhance their party.

Of course, list out your favorite songs that you definitely have to hear and dance to, keeping in mind that songs are an average of three to four minutes long, so don't make a list that will be impossible to play through (more on this later). This should be a relatively short list.

Your "please play" songs are all the rest of your favorite songs. These are songs that will be worked in at appropriate times as time permits.

I started implementing a "only if they beg" song list because I had many couples that would personally cringe at some party songs, but understood after some coaching, that some classic party songs are classics for a reason. I would suggest to them that if there were songs that we would rather avoid, but enough guests really, really wanted them, we would put them on this list. So we wouldn't play them unless begged.

The fourth column would be your "never play" list. These would be the tunes that we would have "accidentally left at home." Because we don't want to hear ex-girlfriend or ex-boyfriend songs or anything like that. Hey, I know we want to show everyone a great time, but it's still your party!

I could go on and write an entire book just on the subject of music programming because I'm so passionate about it, but this chapter is already getting out of control. I hope I was able to shed some light on a topic that is suspiciously absent in many conversations that have to do with successful receptions. You hear a lot about the planning and coordination, which is tremendously important, but let's face it—your guests are going to remember whether they danced up a storm, heard some great music, people watched, or sang along to some great tunes! I consider the music programming to go hand-in-hand with the event coordination by the Master of Ceremonies.

Chapter Five

Seven Essential Truths About DJ Entertainers

every day, couples hire entertainers that they should not be hiring. Planning a wedding reception can be a DIFFICULT and STRESSFUL job. There are so many details that must be attended to. But here is the undeniable truth:

THE OVERALL SUCCESS OF YOUR WEDDING HINGES ON YOU HIRING THE RIGHT DJ ENTERTAINER

Although every detail of wedding planning is important, all of the research and history show that you and your guests will only really remember a handful of details from your reception. When is the last time you remembered the chair covers you saw at a wedding? Did the centerpieces make the event memorable and successful? When is the last time you attended a wedding when what you had for dinner made the event successful? On the other hand, your guests will certainly remember whether they danced like crazy and had a great time. It's a funny thing, but when the DJ Entertainer is "on," people will brag about many things that happen at your reception. But if the DJ is lackluster, it seems like that is the negative word that gets spread around. That being said, you can see the magnitude of responsibility that your DJ Entertainer has!

The DJ Entertainer Is the "Key" to a Successful Event, But Here's the Problem . . .

Hire the wrong person and your wedding can flop. Beware of hiring suspiciously "cheap" entertainment because it can cost you money; it rarely saves you anything. **It costs you more than you think — it won't just cost you the price of the DJ, but what's at stake is actually the entire investment of your wedding!**

After all, if great memories weren't experienced, created, or captured—what did your investment result in?

There are many reasons for this that I will detail for you so you understand the business of DJ Entertainers. Once you understand it, you'll get a better understanding of the economics of the business in order to know when someone may be trying to get one over on you, or merely lacks the experience to know how much is at stake (which is a bad bet for you).

If you hire the wrong entertainer, and your reception isn't successful, there are no do-overs. Those are the memories you will carry for the rest of your lives. If you are capturing your reception in photographs and video, wouldn't you want the best photo opportunities possible?

Before you waste any time calling DJs randomly, take the time to read this report in its entirety. You will benefit by understanding the role a DJ plays at your reception, learn how to find an entertainer that is your best match, and how to avoid the seven costly misconceptions about DJs before you hire one.

Essential DJ Entertainer Truth #1:
Any Fool Can Buy Music and "Push Play," But It's a Genius Who Entertains Using Music That Brings the Best Out of Every Party

There are many, many folks that can pony up the money for really nice equipment and are capable of plugging in and playing some tunes, but few have enough experience in entertaining an audience and organizing the smooth flow of a reception to fill a thimble. This is where you must be very tough minded to discover where your prospective DJ's experience comes from. It is a mistake to think that a person who has only "club" or "corporate" experience can get through a wedding reception.

Now, I'm not saying that a club DJ would not make a great wedding entertainer—it all depends on the extent of their wedding experience! For example, I started my career in the nightclubs, and it was quite a transition when I first started performing at weddings. I had to study the formalities and learn how to do introductions, among many other things. With luck, I managed to get by, but my first few weddings certainly had their kinks. Performing for a nightclub dance floor is wildly different than entertaining for a wedding crowd!

What few people realize is that a nightclub actually only caters to a small percentage of the population—often a party crowd or dance music fans. If you frequent nightclubs, you may agree that besides your friends, you probably don't see your neighbors or the general public there. Well, a wedding reception will consist of mostly people you don't see at nightclubs! This seemingly simple fact just isn't taught at DJ school (I'm joking because most DJs don't go to DJ school), and many people offering DJ services overlook this fact or deem it unimportant.

This is evidenced by many DJ Entertainers who will play ob-scure music and are unfamiliar with remixes of popular songs. This has often puzzled me because songs are popular for a reason, and playing an unrecognizable version of a song will not create an energetic response. And worse, it often causes a visceral reaction from the crowd that wants to hear the original version they love! A nightclub or dance club is often "conditioned" over many weeks and months to love certain remixed versions of songs. A wedding reception crowd obviously wouldn't have that conditioning.

When is a nightclub DJ appropriate for a wedding reception? The answer is, when they have the appropriate wedding experi-ence to know the difference. Plus, there are many celebrity night-club DJs who are hired to perform at wedding receptions for their particular style, but are experienced enough to know the right mix between their style and what the event needs for success.

An inexperienced DJ may be able to get through a simple birth-day party or backyard gathering, but where they really can wreak some havoc is at a wedding reception where timing, organization, and flow are vitally important. Be sure to obtain a list of wedding reception specific references. The best advice I can give you is that whatever DJ or company you hire, you better be sure that there is

Mark with Dr. Drax, the president of
American Disc Jockey Association.

someone there who has a strong track record and understands the fundamentals of organizing and performing wedding receptions.

Essential DJ Entertainer Truth #2:
In Wedding Magazines and Websites, They Put DJs
Under "Music." However, Your DJ Entertainer's Role Is
More Than Just "Music."

Sure, the wedding magazines and websites need a simple label to put on a DJ Entertainer, so it's easy to see why they almost always label them as "music." They have a category for "wedding planners," but they typically do not make the announcements during the reception, even if you were to hire one. More accurately, your DJ will be entirely responsible for the smooth flow of your reception. Your DJ Entertainer will be your entertainment director and reception event coordinator, who will **create and execute the agenda for the entire evening**. This role is especially amplified if you are not using the services of a wedding consultant. If you are using a wedding planner/consultant, typically you would want your DJ Entertainer to work closely with your planner. Since your DJ Entertainer will have the microphone as your Master of Ceremonies, they are the person with their finger on the pulse of every formality, activity, and have first-hand communication with other vendors. Often, your DJ Entertainer can help your wedding planner avoid timeline conflicts, make suggestions, and offer fresh ideas for enhancing the experience.

You will benefit from the experience of a wedding entertainment DJ professional. They will be able to guide you through all the formalities and give you suggestions to make your day unique and unforgettable. A great entertainer will also use their expertise to incorporate your ideas and suggestions into the program. But don't just hire a "yes" man. Be sure that the entertainer is giving you the real scoop, and not just telling you what he thinks you want to hear.

Essential DJ Entertainer Truth #3:
Of Course Price Is Important, But Beware
Of the Suspiciously Cheap DJ

Wow, this is a biggie. Of course, price is a factor when hiring your DJ, but don't let it be the single deciding factor. Is the highest-priced performer always the best? Not necessarily. On the other hand, hiring the least expensive entertainer can be dangerous if you're not aware of the hidden "gotchas."Once you know the economics of this business, you will better understand how to identify a safe, reliable professional from a potentially high-risk choice. We will give you a crash-course in valuing a DJ Entertainer so you can have a behind-the-curtain look at what *really* goes on behind the price.

We understand that, for many brides, hiring a DJ Entertainer is a new experience. By now, you may have already learned that there is a lot going on behind the curtain. You have probably learned enough not to mistakenly think of DJs as a "dime a dozen," or a commodity. Fees for DJ Entertainers have a wide range across the country, from less than $1,000 on the low end to $5,000 and up for a complete wedding reception. The most common fees in major metropolitan areas are in the $1,400 to $2,500 range. When is a DJ Entertainer the right price? Why are some fees higher than others? Are their services really so different? An entertainer's popularity is one factor, but there are other factors.

There are a few things to consider.... The fact is that each DJ Entertainer is unique. Like every profession, there are some DJs who are great, others who are mediocre, and others who should never be allowed to perform! You need to decide on the performer that is most qualified to perform your reception, that you are comfortable with (since the DJ will be representing you and your family), and that has the proper experience and credentials. Understand that DJs should not be hired by price alone and BEWARE of "suspiciously cheap" DJs, there may be a reason for it. To illustrate this point, consider this true story:

$300 DJ Ruins $30,000 Wedding Reception

This is an actual story that affected a family member of one of my past clients, and I will reveal exactly why it occurs. The sad news is that it occurs all too often, and could be avoided if the world got their hands on this book!

My DJ Entertainer business is considered on the higher end of the price range in my market. The folks who become my clients are often experienced in hiring entertainment and already know what to look for. By the time they've come to me, they may have already been stung in the past by a bad experience or know someone very close who has. In one of my final consultations with a couple, they shared a heart-wrenching story with me about the bride's sister's wedding reception that they wish they could forget.

I'll give you the punch line first, but it's not funny at all... The DJ was a no-show! She had been sold a DJ for $300 by a company that unethically (in my opinion) tells brides what they are hoping to hear in an effort to win their contract. They essentially say, "Listen, you're looking for music, right? I've got all the songs—are those expensive DJs going to give you more that is worth four or five times what I charge?" They simply promote DJ service as a commodity and do their business by volume. For those innocent brides that fall for that pitch, they don't realize the risks they are taking. I'm going to let you in on a deep, dark secret that I haven't seen anyone have the guts to reveal before:

In our industry, there is a term that we use: bottom-feeders. They exist in every industry, but they do a lot of damage in ours. Here's why...

What they do is sell people on a cheap price and then find someone later that they can subcontract the job to. What these bottom feeders do is call other DJs in their area, looking for desperate, unbooked DJs that would agree to take the job! This may work okay for hotels selling unsold rooms at a discount, but this can be a disaster for something as personalized as a wedding reception, as you might imagine.

How do I know? I've gotten these calls, and they still happen to this day. I would get a call from a DJ, basically asking if I had any DJs available for "this Saturday" (that's how last-minute they are). Then they would make an offer, something like, **"I only charged $300, so if you could do it for $150, it's yours . . . I've collected $150, so you get the balance from the bride and you keep it."** Is that not the scariest thing you've ever heard? It happens all the time, even in today's web-wired world.

What happened to my client's sister was that the bottom feeder couldn't fulfill all of his commitments, and they just didn't have a DJ who could show up for that night. What's most offensive is their flippant attitude about it all. I've heard a bottom feeder say that they consider it a successful month if they have fewer than 2 "screamers." Yes, that's the derogatory term that they have coined to describe brides they knowingly let down and expect complaint calls from on Monday!

So Then, What Is the Right Price for a DJ Entertainer?

A professional DJ Entertainer who is pricing and valuing their service will consider a number of factors to determine their rate. I can't speak for them individually, but I can give you the things a professional has to consider if they want to assure top-notch service to their clients:

The DJ Entertainer's Popularity and Demand—As the old saying goes, supply and demand are key factors that drive price. This is a talent-driven business, and out of the thousands of people that hang out their shingle and offer their services as a DJ, it is a tiny percentage that would be considered top tier. This principle applies whether you are considering a multi-operator DJ company or a solo operator DJ. The best in both classes will be booked solid, often 6 to 18 months in advance. By the way, this suggests that you should secure your DJ Entertainer as early in your planning as possible.

Operating Costs and Safety Backup—One big trap that may be obvious to people in the business, but less obvious to first time consumers, is the simple fact that a DJ Entertainer typically wants to operate at a profit and make a living. At a bare minimum, the DJ Entertainer has a number of fixed costs and overhead items, including new music purchase, gas/travel, dry cleaning, marketing, rent, labor (for assistants, office, etc.), equipment maintenance, backup systems, and more. The takeaway here is that the lower the price a DJ promotes themselves for actually reveals that they are going to sacrifice other aspects of service (or they're simply unaware), putting the client at ultimate risk. As example, if a piece of equipment breaks, would a DJ have the profit needed for proper replacement? Or will the next client go without? Very few people can be happy performing at a loss. As an aside, I often overpay when I'm hiring people, especially for a critical task. I'm not suggesting that you need to do the same, but I'm just sharing my philosophy that I want people I work with to be the happiest people on the planet, so I want to take away any excuse within my control so they are extra-thrilled to please me!

Operating Costs Going Beyond Their Time On-site—Your celebration may start at the time you listed on your invitation, may that be 6 PM or 7 PM for cocktails, but for your DJ Entertainer, it should start much earlier. For 6 PM cocktail hour, your DJ Entertainer doesn't just want to be on time, they have to be early. They must allow at least one hour to nicely and cleanly install their equipment, organize and clean their area, and test their sound and lights so your first guest hears perfection. Personally, I prefer to arrive two hours before guests are expected.

Your DJ Entertainer must also take into consideration their travel time and the time it takes to load their truck, then unload the truck into the venue. Before they load their truck, they will double-check their music inventory and cross-reference it with your formality requirements and play lists. It is not uncommon for a DJ Entertainer to begin their day at 12 noon for an event that begins at 6 PM. If they have an assistant, their labor considerations begin at noon, not just at the time your reception begins.

Many of my clients have found my DJ preparation checklist instructive, so I've included it here. This will give you a behind-the-scenes look at how a DJ Entertainer prepares for your wedding reception. The reason why bottom feeder DJs are a very risky investment is because they will have to shortcut many of the preparation steps outlined below in order to "feel" profitable.

Mark Imperial's Wedding Reception Entertainment Time Commitment

Although it appears that you are purchasing a five- or six-hour wedding package, this is the time allotted to create and perform an

Imperial Signature Celebration!

Total Time Commitment: 35–58 hours

PERSONAL CONSULTATION WITH YOUR MASTER OF CEREMONIES 3–4 hours

We have the most comprehensive planning in the industry, covering all aspects of your reception from the entrance of your first guest until the final goodbye. Designed to allow you to enjoy your reception, stress-free, we will take care of everything.

PERSONALIZED TIMELINE/AGENDA FOR ENTIRE RECEPTION 2–3 hours

We will create the agenda and coordinate with all other vendors, including the venue, photographer, and videographer, so that everything runs smoothly and you will always have the special moments captured on film. The detailed agenda will be based upon our consultation together, and assures you that all professional vendors will be working as a team to create your ideal reception.

FINALIZATION OF DETAILS WITH MASTER OF CEREMONIES AND TRAVEL 4–8 hours

Your Master of Ceremonies will coordinate with the bride, groom, parents, grandparents, and anyone giving toasts or special traditions. Contact will be by phone or in person. Once these details are finalized, a finalization meeting is scheduled with the bride and groom. These highly detailed meetings are necessary to assure a smooth reception.

CUSTOM INTRODUCTIONS AND LOVE STORIES 6–8 hours

Your Master of Ceremonies will create a personalized introduction for you and your special guests and/or your own unique love story set to music. They can be funny, romantic, emotional, or more often, a combination of all three.

CUSTOM RECORDINGS 4–8 hours

We offer a variety of custom recording options. The bride and groom can record special messages to each other, which we will edit to perfection and master into the first dance. We will also remaster the music to customize the instrumental portions to fit your words perfectly. You may also choose a message from the bride to her father for the father/daughter dance, from bride and groom to their parents or guests, the vows from the ceremony, messages from guests unable to attend, or many other variations.

PRE-RECEPTION COORDINATION 1–2 hours

On location, we will coordinate with all your other vendors prior to the reception to iron out every small detail. Additional photography, special arrivals, toasts, or presentations will be orchestrated into the evening smoothly.

EVENT PREPARATION, TRAVEL, SET UP, AND STRIKE TIME 5–10 hours

Behind the scenes, normal preparation on the day of your reception begins five to ten hours prior to start time. The equipment and backup is double-checked, truck is loaded, props and specialty items are prepared, and our arrival is scheduled between two to three hours prior to your first guest arrival. Equipment is set up and tested along with microphones, so that the first guest hears perfection.

ON-SITE STAFF/ PRODUCTION ASSISTANT 10–18 hours

Our production assistant is another DJ who helps your Master of Ceremonies. This allows your MC to leave the DJ booth to coordinate with the family, wedding party, vendors, or guests.

EVENT PERFORMANCE 5–6 hours

From the moment of your first guest arrival to the final goodnight, we will deliver a lifetime of memories, using the highest quality entertainment, music, sound, and lighting. We will manage our 100-point checklist and assure you the most memorable and successful wedding reception ever.

As you've discovered, the work that begins well before the big day is easily overlooked and often misunderstood!

Here is a tip that can help you determine your DJ Entertainer budget...

Instead of starting by pricing out DJ Entertainers, decide on a price range that you can afford, then check out a few in that range, and choose the best performer. Professional DJ rates are all over the board. They range from under $1,000 to over $5,000 for a complete reception, and are based on the DJ's popularity, demand, and availability.

Even at the top of the range, it still tops out at the cost of a good live band, making DJ Entertainers a great value, and also explains why they are a popular choice. Considering the fact that the DJ is responsible for over 80% of the success of your wedding reception, it warrants more priority than the less-memorable elements at the reception, like chair covers, wouldn't you agree?

Wedding websites and magazines report on "average budgets" spent on individual elements of wedding planning, with "music" being one of those parts. The numbers can be misleading because the surveys given post-wedding show that over 80% of brides reported they would have spent more on their entertainment, had they realized beforehand that it was such an integral part of their reception. Nevertheless, the surveys showed that brides spent between 5 to 10% of the entire wedding budget on their entertainment. I have a more pragmatic suggestion, with an unconventional example for illustration...

Considering your favorite band could rock a party in an empty warehouse, you could spend as much as you wanted on your favorite band and serve bread and water! I know, I know, I'm just being dramatic, but for many reasons, using the "percentage of wedding budget" formula doesn't seem useful.

I recommend you take a practical look at how much you value the "experience" vs. the "stuff," and spend as much as you are comfortable with. If you want to use the "percentage of budget" formula knowing what you know now, you can bump up that percentage to between 8% and 20% of your entire wedding budget for your entertainment.

Essential DJ Entertainer Truth #4:
DJ Entertainers Are often Booked 12 to 24 Months Ahead, So You Should Act as Soon as Possible When You Know Your Date

When I consult with a bride, I will ask her how the other aspects of the planning are coming along to see if I can be of any help to her, or offer my knowledge. Since I need to work with other vendors, I'll ask who was booked for photography and videography, for example. Surprisingly, I often hear, "I'm going to use (vendor's name) because he/she does great work; I haven't booked them yet, but I'm going to." I then ask them if they know whether that vendor is still available for their date, and they reply, "Oh, I haven't thought of that." More than a few times, the bride discovers that she missed booking a vendor by overlooking that fact. It made me wonder how often this happens with DJ Entertainers simply because of this oversight.

It's more important to book early in the DJ Entertainer category because often you want a specific entertainer or company. With photographers and videographers, when you are working with boutique specialists and artists, this is also vital. The more popular your performer or vendor, the harder they will be to lock-in, and why you should act as soon as you know your date.

Every year, I get a number of calls from brides in a "panic." For one reason or another, they cannot find a DJ Entertainer available for their date. Even worse, I have heard more than a few brides say that the DJ they got "through a friend" has disappeared and left them in the lurch. What makes this even scarier is that now their choices have gone from "who is the best DJ for them" to being forced to hire whoever may be available. With no time left to research, and with so many other details hanging over them, finding the right DJ will be more about random luck than educated decision. As I mentioned earlier in the book, the $300 DJ can ruin the $30,000 reception simply because their low price can be an indicator of their low priority. It is more likely that these suspiciously low-priced bottom feeders become "no shows" and disappear. Some folks mean well but are ill-prepared to follow through on commitments. Don't let this happen to you.

The truth is, the best, most popular DJ Entertainers will be booked more than six to twelve months in advance, in some cases up to two or three years. If you begin your entertainment research early enough, and you discover a great entertainer, don't think that he will be available if you call weeks later. It is difficult enough to find that perfect entertainer—the one who makes you comfortable, someone you like, and who understands your tastes. It only makes sense that you secure your date right away with a written agreement. In most cases, DJs see their calendar as their "inventory" and cannot hold a date without a written agreement and a retainer.

Essential DJ Entertainer Truth #5:
Because a Wedding Reception Is A Live, In-Person Event, Meet Face-to-Face with Your DJ Entertainer Whenever Possible

In today's Internet world, many people have been conditioned to shop online. There is nothing wrong with that in many cases; however, remember that your wedding reception is going to be a live, in-person affair and that you will want to be very comfortable with your choice of spokesperson/DJ Entertainer/Master of Ceremonies. You can feel comfortable with a person by phone, but nothing beats meeting with them in person. Once you meet your entertainer by phone, be sure you immediately set an in-person meeting. When meeting with your vendors, you should always bring all decision-makers to the meeting, and there is an important reason why:

Your DJ Entertainer's experience and knowledge are available for you to learn from, and for all of your decision-makers' benefit, they should all be present to have all of their ideas, questions, and concerns heard and answered. There will be exciting ideas that come up at the meeting, and you will want to take advantage of the time you will have with the professionals you are meeting with.

Also, you want all of your decision makers to experience the entire meeting with your prospective vendors. In my experience, it adds undue stress to have to reschedule unnecessary additional meetings. People can't make informed decisions secondhand, they need to be there. It makes everyone more comfortable.

Plus, your DJ Entertainer will likely be working very close with you, so you will benefit from them meeting your family right from the beginning.

It is also better to meet with your prospective DJ Entertainer in private rather than during another client's wedding reception.

Auditioning a DJ at another bride's wedding has long been a controversial subject. I will put it in a logical perspective here and give you the real scoop. Simply ask yourself if you would like strangers walking into your reception (often in street clothes) for the purpose of seeing one of your vendors? It is not the proper time or place to audition a DJ. There are several reasons why it is not even useful for anyone involved.

First, it is an obviously uncomfortable position for both the wedding party and the visiting prospect. Uninvited guests stand out like a sore thumb and are an un-welcomed distraction. Second, unless a prospect sees the entire reception, they won't get the big picture experience. Also, they are seeing someone else's unique wedding, and unless the DJ is of the "cookie cutter" variety, the prospect again will get no value without knowing what is unique. Third and most importantly, it creates a "split loyalty" from the DJ.

The DJ may do things out of place just to show off for their prospect, when they should be focusing 100% on appropriate timing for their current client. This is my opinion on the subject; however, I still see many performers and live bands "auditioning" for new prospects at other client's receptions.

There are better ways to audition your DJ. The right time should be one on one, at a private consultation. A professional wedding DJ should be able to show you weddings they have performed or paint you an accurate picture while they are right beside you to explain each and every detail. This also allows you to see all the different formalities and unique elements of their performance without crashing someone else's wedding and holding up the walls for five hours. You will also have your prospective DJ Entertainer's undivided attention.

Essential DJ Entertainer Truth #6:
Not Every DJ Entertainer Experience Qualifies Them to Perform for Wedding Receptions

A very common misconception is that any experienced DJ should be able to perform for a wedding reception. A wedding reception has many elements that need to be coordinated, and you really must know that your prospective DJ Entertainer has lots of wedding-specific experience. I had been a hotmix and nightclub DJ for many years before I performed my first wedding. I had the good fortune of having an experienced wedding professional accompany me on the job and walk me through all of the formalities. Without him, I might have missed a formality! Not everyone is as fortunate. The lesson is to be sure that the DJ Entertainer you are considering has specific experience with the type of party you are planning. Whether it's a wedding reception, Bar or Bat Mitzvah, or other type of celebration that involves formalities or special traditions, it requires a professional who is entirely experienced with those formalities.

The great DJ Entertainer could be the life of the party, but you wouldn't want them to forget the Horah at a Bar Mitzvah, and they'll need to know the difference between the Motzi and the Kiddush. Same with wedding receptions—it is very easy to take the grand entrance for granted, but a DJ Entertainer who underestimates the preparation can turn it into an awkward introduction.

Another unspoken truth is that many nightclub DJs are not accustomed to using the microphone! Now, I want to be clear, there are lots of nightclub DJs who have tons of wedding experience as well, but you will want to know that for sure.

When I was playing predominantly at nightclubs, I was approached many times by happy, excited couples who would say, "You MUST DJ our wedding," but they didn't realize that a wedding reception and a nightclub are two different animals.

It was easier for me to adapt because I was at a "Showtime" nightclub run by Walter Payton's company. We had pioneered the Showtime follow-along dances and line dances at nightclubs, so I was one of the few DJ Entertainers who were also stage performers. Still, I was very nervous not being familiar with the timeline of a wedding reception at the time and all of the other vendors looking to me for direction. As I mentioned, I had the foresight to bring an experienced wedding professional with me to answer any of my questions and keep me on the ball for all of the formalities. With luck, I did okay, and the party rocked, but the timeline was a little stiff because it was the first time I ever ran them. After hundreds of killer wedding receptions, an experienced DJ Entertainer will rock the timeline with natural flair.

Work with a specialist in the type of party you are planning, like your wedding reception.

Essential DJ Entertainer Truth #7:
Wedding Receptions Can Be as Unique as the Couple

No two wedding receptions need to be alike. They don't need to be "cookie-cutter." Your reception represent the first time you and your spouse are throwing a gathering as husband and wife. It should be an extension of your personality and style. A big mistake is allowing an entertainer to do their usual "schtick," making your day a carbon copy of every other wedding for the year.

How are you sure the DJ will make your day unique? Simply see if he or she asks you what you are looking for. Be wary of the DJ that just touts his music list and achievements. See if they ask you what you are looking for first, and then offer you the right solutions to make your day special.

Bonus Essential DJ Entertainer Truth:
It Takes a Talented DJ Entertainer to Make
Your Soundtrack Magic

The most talented DJ Entertainers I have ever heard understand the power of a song. They know that songs must be chosen wisely. In an hour of party time, you can only hear an average of 15 songs. That's 45 songs in three hours of dancing. A really great DJ

Entertainer knows how to make those 45 songs count.

A really talented DJ also knows how to approach current songs, but they know the greatest responses will be from an old song. Why? There's something magical about an old song. A great song carries memories for each and every guest. One awesome song played at just the right moment creates a rush of emotions—you know how the crowd roars at a concert? When that mix is just right, you'll laugh, you'll cry, you'll be touched in some way. What will your soundtrack sound like?

* * *

Well, there you have it. I hope you have discovered the importance of hiring the right entertainer and why you should give it your highest priority. You may have known some of the secrets revealed in this chapter, but I hope you found a few gems that you can use to ensure that your reception turns out exactly as you want it so you get all the fun, excitement, and memories that your family deserves and will cherish forever.

Chapter Six

Your DJ Entertainer Hiring Checklist

Now it's time to get serious and choose the right DJ Entertainer for you! Here's a quick checklist for you, so you know what to do in order, and what you should pay close attention to.

1. BOOK YOUR DJ AS EARLY AS YOU KNOW YOUR DATE. Since the most popular DJ Entertainers are often booked 12 months in advance or more, you'll want to put this at the top of your priority list next to booking your venue. DJs consider their dates as their "inventory" so they can't economically hold any dates without a commitment.

2. MAKE SURE YOUR DJ ENTERTAINER USES A CONTRACT TO PROTECT BOTH PARTIES. A professional contract will help you sleep at night knowing that you've taken care of business, and protect you against any hidden surprises. Most entertainers only require a small retainer along with a written agreement to lock in your date. Although different entertainers offer unique packages to choose from, what's more important is that you lock your date when you know the DJ or the company you want to work with. Simply tell them that you want to work with them and that you want to give them a retainer and lock your date with an agreement, even if you're undecided on the package. Just let them know that you will make the package decision later, but that it is important to you that you can work with them. Most companies will appreciate this and be more than happy to accommodate your request.

3. ASK YOUR DJ HOW EARLY THEY WILL ARRIVE ON YOUR BIG DAY. Perhaps it should go without saying, but even though it may take less than a half hour to set up and test a sound system, you'll want to know that they allow plenty of time for a sound check and organization. If your entertainer is including a lighting package, that will take more time, so find their policies on setup time.

4. ASK ABOUT THEIR EQUIPMENT AND BACKUP PLAN. Although talent, expertise, and musical abilities come first, the sound and lighting systems are the tools your DJ will use to perform. An experienced entertainer's top priority is maintaining trouble-free equipment. This is important because it will allow them to focus their creative energy on your music and entertainment. They should have a backup plan in place in case of any technical breakdown. There are many ways to be protected with a backup system. Computer-based DJ technology has come so far that an entertainer can carry a spare laptop, hard drive, or even CD players. Your DJ can share with you how they protect themselves against surprises or breakdowns.

Chapter Seven

How to Make Sure Your DJ Rocks the House

Now that you've booked your wedding reception's most important vendor, did you know there is a way to make sure to get the best performance from them? In this chapter, I'll share with you what I've learned over the years working with my own DJ Entertainers and clients.

1. Is Your DJ as Stress-free as the Bride and Groom Should Be?
One of the biggest determining factors as to whether a DJ is going to rock or not, is whether they are in a good mood or not. A lot of this you will have to read in their personality when you book them. I'm not suggesting that you need to coddle them or babysit them, but rather, you will want to know their demeanor in general. Are they calm, cool, and collected? They can still be outrageous and fun

(if that's what you want), but they have to demonstrate that they can handle high-pressure situations with the coolness of a relief pitcher in baseball—being put into the ballgame with bases loaded, no outs, the tying run on third base, and the winning run on second! Be sure you genuinely like that DJ as a person so you will be able to communicate any challenges or concerns without having to be adversarial. This way, you would have no reason to cause confrontation or otherwise strain the relationship. Your DJ is there to please you; just have open communication and let them know what will make you happy. Your DJ really does get more gratification from making you happy. It's not the money, it's seeing you happy that is truly the reward for a DJ in this business, because it's a passion.

As a rule of thumb, I did everything I could to make sure that my crew was in a good mood when we would go into a party. What I found was, the more prepared we were, and the more rehearsed we were, the better mood we were in. The crowd truly feeds off the DJ's energy, and if the DJs are in an awesome mood, you're virtually guaranteed a rockin' good time. The tips in this chapter will allow you and your DJ Entertainer to be the most prepared ever so you can be in a great mood for your big day.

2. Come Up with Some Milestones Together

Have a clear understanding of when you're expected to have your forms completed and turned in. You can decide with your DJ what the best time would be to have your final arrangements meeting. Personally, I like to have this meeting no more than two or three weeks before the big day. I prefer this because tastes and things change. It's pretty safe that within two weeks before your big day, the music and the plans you finalized will still feel good.

Line around the building to see Mark host.

3. How to Communicate with Your DJ Entertainer for Best Results

Each entertainer has a system for communicating and planning. Many DJ companies incorporate online planning systems on their websites that make it super simple to communicate with your entertainer in one place. You'll want to make sure you understand their expectations and set clear guidelines for when to have those online planning documents completed. Over my years of observation, the number one cause of party breakdown is over-communication. It is best to carry a notebook or page labeled "talk with DJ," and every time you get an idea or thought, you can write it in this notebook. Then, on your next scheduled call with your DJ, you can go over that page with them. This method has worked great for me over the years, and because the communication happens in chunks, it makes it much easier to remember all the details. What used to happen was the client would call each time they had an idea, or when a song just popped up into their mind. What you should realize is that your DJ will receive this in little pieces, which often doesn't communicate well into your client file. Picture a desk or wall covered with little sticky notes—that is what it's like when a client calls every time they get one idea. A slight breeze blows, and they're all over the place. This is how the tiny details slip through the cracks. Don't let tiny details slip through the cracks! Put all of your talking points on a page in a notebook, and handle them during your final arrangements meeting.

4. Tell Your DJ about Any Uncommon Plans for Implementation Suggestions

You may have a really unique and cool idea, and you may want to keep it a secret, but don't have any secrets with your DJ Entertainer! Your DJ is there to help you, so use their expertise and experience to deploy your idea. They may even help you avert any potential hidden traps. I have an example for you: Long ago, around 1990, before you and I used the Internet, a couple bought one of the early video phones and thought it would be neat to make a call to grandma in Israel during the wedding reception! Yes, that was a super cool idea at the time. The family even communicated that with their wedding planner. For whatever reason, that particular wedding planner didn't find it necessary to mention it to the DJ (us). Instead, they showed up at the reception with the videophone still in the box and said, "Hook this up so we can call Israel sometime during dinner; this will be so cool!" I nearly turned white because my technician brain told me we were going to have problems. I'm not a phone technician, but I know that commercial buildings have this thing called "PBX" where all the phone lines are routed through a proprietary brain. This meant that it would not have a conventional phone line available, rendering this idea useless. Of course, technical things like this are not common knowledge, so I can understand the wedding planner not foreseeing any potential problems. This example suggests that when you're trying to do anything that involves technology, simply talk about it with your DJ in advance! Although I'm not a phone technician, I am a gearhead, which most people in our field are. They know enough to be dangerous, but they're also astute enough to plan ahead and ask for advice. In this case, given enough notice, we could have heard from grandma.

5. Consult with Your DJ About Their Music Request Formula

Another huge cause of potential breakdown is the music play list. An experienced DJ Entertainer will coach you through the importance of your playlist and how you should think about your requests. Although each individual DJ will handle this differently, I will give you some of the big talking points here. First of all, the unshakable truths: Let's suppose a song has an average length of 3 1/2 minutes. That would mean you could play only 17 songs in an hour—and that's if you played them back to back with no pause for announcements at all. We know there will be announcements, formalities, and other fun, so let's set a rule of thumb that we can play 15 songs per hour. Now let's just talk about the dancing after dinner: If that's three hours, you'll only have time to hear 45 songs. A common breakdown in communication happens when a bride is not given a guideline about making requests and returns with a playlist that is 250 songs long. That's a 14-hour long playlist, not taking into consideration any formalities or programming format. It's not the bride's fault, because that's not common knowledge, and people do not typically think that way. This is an educational process. Let's breakdown that hour even further...

6. Rules of Thumb for Your Playlist and Guest Requests

DJ Entertainers have a variety of ways to go about handling requests; I will share mine: Remember we talked about only being able to hear about 15 songs per hour? We also have to take into consideration there will be guests making requests on the fly. Will you allow your DJ to take your guests' requests? This is a real consideration. Next we have to accommodate for special announcements or planned activities because this is a social affair and not a nightclub. Then, your DJ needs some room to do his magic. This means that he will use his musical knowledge and programming skills to play perfect transition songs that will turn your playlist into a fantastic voyage! These transition songs, classics, and recurrent hits are vitally important in setting the mood and engaging your guests to dance with the magic that music brings. Knowing we have to fit all that into the hour, what is the reasonable number of songs to request? Surprisingly, this makes your job even simpler. I recommend to my clients that they focus on requesting one third of the songs per hour, so the rule of thumb is five songs per party hour. This actually helps you, because you can make that your "must play"killer songs per hour. In this example, for a five-hour reception, you can make a 25 song "must play" list. This way you are assured to hear your favorite songs, and you will avoid unnecessary disappointment due to unrealistic expectations. I then tell my clients to make a "rest of the best" list, which is a list of songs that they'd like to hear when there's time. Your DJ Entertainer will go to this list, and oftentimes find the killer transition songs here, so everyone's a winner! I'm teaching you a lot of the killer tips, tricks, and secrets that I share with my own staff and DJ students around the world.

The last short list I asked my clients to create is a "do not play" list. These are the songs that they absolutely wish would never exist no matter what. I take this list a step further; I call it the "only-if-they-beg" subset of the list. Basically, I have my clients put a star next to songs on their "do not play" list that would be allowed if the crowd really pressed. During final arrangements, we'll have a discussion about this list, just to make sure we're all on the same page. So here, in a nutshell, are the three lists you should make: 1) Must Play List 2) The Rest of the Best 3) Do Not Play w/ a subset list of "Only if they beg."

In Summary

If I were to summarize the two big takeaways from this chapter, I would say for one, be sure to set your expectations with your DJ Entertainer from the beginning. Discuss your goals, set realistic deadlines for your planning guides to be completed, and set a final arrangements meeting where you will go over all of your notes. Keep a good set of notes, but don't feel you have to call your DJ every time you have an idea because it's better to give it to them all at once. If you have a simple technical question, or just wonder if something can be done realistically, you can call your DJ. Call them for clarifying questions, but save the big items and planning elements for your final arrangements meeting.

Secondly, set realistic expectations for your music playlist. If you follow the "rules of thumb guidelines" I suggested above, you'll be in great shape. These guidelines will give your DJ Entertainer everything needed to be well-prepared without over preparation. Have a great time and rock the house!

Chapter Eight

Can I DJ My Own Wedding Reception Using an iPod?

Take This Test...

This bonus chapter is meant to help you determine whether or not you would want to attempt to perform as a DJ entertainer and master of ceremonies for your own wedding reception. You've probably seen articles in wedding magazines and websites promoting the DIY approach to your "music" using an iPod.

Here, I'm going to give you the unvarnished truth, show you what it takes, and point out the big, hidden "gotchas" so you can avoid them if you are considering doing this yourself.

This chapter is not meant to turn you into a sound engineer or give you a degree in sound engineering. Instead, I've included the BIG things to look for when setting up your sound system. Although no amount of reading books will substitute for experience, this chapter is meant to minimize the surprises!

You may wonder why a book written by DJ entertainers would want to include information like this. The simple fact is that our passion as DJ entertainers really comes from seeing people succeed with their wedding receptions. Since we have the knowledge and experience from both the technical side and the entertainment side, we can give you accurate reporting without coloring the facts in any way. To tell you the truth, true professional DJ entertainers are there to serve the right clients, not everyone. I would suggest to be cautious around anyone who would try to steer you either way. In everything we do, we believe in simply reporting the facts and letting you decide. Here are a few bullet points that you should consider if you're thinking about the DIY approach...

Will your reception require any special announcements? I've attended some very nice, small receptions that were simply meant to be lunch-only or dinner-only. These were second or third marriages and a small, intimate family-only gathering. They were held at restaurants with just dinner tables. In fact, some were completely absent of master of ceremonies or music; the typical restaurant overhead music remained. If this is all you're doing, and you imagine it feeling just like a night out at a nice restaurant, then hiring a DJ may not be necessary. An iPod may not even be necessary. But if you are planning any announcements at all, or if you will need to organize people in any way, you need to consider who that organizer will be, who won't be upset about being asked to work.

Will your venue require speakers? If so, you can rent them. There are many music stores that rent speakers. When you call them, you'll want to be specific about "PA speakers." "PA" stands for public address. These speakers are specifically designed for larger spaces and will carry the sound further with cleaner audio. They also handle the higher power requirements needed.

Some people make the mistake of using home stereo equipment, thinking it is all the same, but it is not. Home stereo equipment, although it sounds great in your house, falls apart in larger spaces. It is meant to be listened to in closer proximity. What you'll find is the more you turn up the volume, the more distortions you'll hear. Plus, the sound will not travel any further because the speaker cones themselves are not designed for that purpose. Public address speakers are built with horns that are specifically designed for long throw.

What to look for in your Sound System Setup . . .

Like I said, many music stores and rental facilities have public address speakers available for rent. You'll have to do a little bit of homework to know which brands and models to look for.

You will need two more things: 1) source mixer 2) amplification. The source mixer is required so you have a place to plug your iPod or CD player into. Keep in mind that many speakers are not designed to have inputs, but to merely act as monitors that accept speaker leads. The speaker leads will come from the amplifier.

Some amplifiers are only designed to accept a single master input. These types of amplifiers are designed to accept inputs from a source mixer (or a pre-amp). The source mixer, or pre-amp, is the place where you would plug in everything that you want to play. This is where you can control the levels of each piece of source equipment independently and create a "mix." You would plug in your iPod and your microphone here.

Now, some speaker systems have built-in amplifiers, which are commonly called "powered speakers." These are good because they eliminate the need for an extra amplifier; however, be aware that they will need to be placed near an electrical outlet or you will be running extension cords. These extension cords should be taped down using stage tape, also available at music stores. Stage tape is different than duct tape. It is designed not to ruin cords, carpet, or floor. You will want to keep this in mind so you don't run into any trouble with your venue!

Some powered speakers even have built-in preamps or mixers. These may or may not be the best solution for you if you want to place the iPod and control everything from a table away from the speaker. What will happen is, you may have seen some powered speakers with a wire hanging down an iPod hanging in the air. This is because somebody used the built-in preamp of the powered speaker. I'm pointing this out because it ends up being awkward.

Let's suppose you are using powered speakers with a separate source mixer or preamp. This is a nice setup for a smaller reception, where you don't necessarily want to "rock the house." I recommend that you ask the rental facility to go over each and every input with you in person. This is because there are so many different combinations of cables and inputs, that if you were missing just one specific type of input, it would render the entire system inoperable!

Just as a quick reference, most iPods use 1/8" stereo plugs (2 rings). Most home stereo CD players will use RCA. You will also run into XLR connectors and 1/4" stereo plugs. There are also mono versions of both 1/8" and 1/4" (single ring plug). Some components will use HDMI, others will use USB. Some digital gear won't talk to analog gear. You need to know this because one of the biggest surprises for most people who don't do this for a living is that they have gotten all incompatible gear. If you don't want to learn all this stuff, consult with a professional to avoid disappointment.

Again, I don't expect you to get a sound engineering degree, but this is meant to bring you awareness so you know what to look for and what to ask from your rental facility.

You could have the rental center deliver and set up your gear to avoid surprises... If any of this technical mumbo jumbo sounds intimidating to you, your best bet may be to have an experienced rental vendor set it up for you. This would hold them accountable for making sure you are good to go. Be very careful, because I've seen rental centers drop-off equipment without enough cables to run the show. Cables, by the way, are some of the biggest items on a DJ entertainer's technical checklist; many cables are not commonly available in stores should an emergency occur.

Rental rates range... Typically, rental centers price everything piece by piece, à la carte. They will give you a price for the mixer preamp, another price for the amplifier, and a per-speaker price. Don't forget the wireless microphones. Wireless microphones typically rent for around $100 each. Most places won't nickel and dime you for cables, they will usually be included. You should be able to put an entire sound system together for a rental rate of less than $750, including one wireless microphone, and sometimes including delivery.

In my DJ business, I actually offer a "DJ system in a box," and it includes everything you need for a nice size reception, complete with wireless microphone and a system simplified for almost anyone to be able to operate. A good reason for renting from a DJ company is because sound systems and lighting systems are their life, so you're sure to have all the bases covered. You can't say that about a typical rental center, where the employees are not DJs, but warehouse staff. At the rental center, the sound equipment is just another piece of inventory, and usually a very small part. They make most of their money renting tables and chairs. It would make me nervous to take sound system advice from them.

What about your lighting? Lighting really sets the mood and energizes the dancing, so you may want to consider renting lights as well. You may be surprised to learn that the lighting systems can be more complicated and time-consuming to set up than the sound. You'll want to allow yourself double the time for setup. If you allow an hour to set up sound, you should allow an additional hour for lighting. Depending on the type and amount of lighting you want to rent, the rental fees range between $100 to over $1,000 for higher-end lighting systems, plus delivery.

Watch your contract! Many things change, so be sure that your rental contract will protect you in case you change your mind. For example, if you decide that all of the details about your MC and music become overwhelming to you, you want to be sure you can cancel your rental without penalty. In my DJ business, for example, what I've done to protect my rental clients is allow them 100% full credit towards a complete DJ entertainer package, should they become overwhelmed up to 30 days prior to their date. Of course, this is dependent on availability, as we're often booked out 12 to 18 months in advance.

Sometimes DIY isn't cost-effective, depending on your application. For a very small function, the rental of under $500 may work out just fine for you. People sometimes look at do-it-yourself as "free," but there is a cost, as you have read. There are rental considerations. When I travel as a DJ to perform at corporate events, I incur these rental fees myself.

For the average-size wedding, you may find that getting full-service from a professional DJ Entertainer can take all of these details off of your shoulders for a fee that is a greater value than the rental alone. Why? The big surprise is that most DJ companies don't charge you for their equipment. This is like hiring a landscaper versus renting the tools. DJ companies' tools are included with their services. The only upgrade consideration is typically for high-end lighting upgrades, which require additional resources and labor to deliver.

I hope this bonus chapter has been enlightening to you and gives you ultimate awareness about the big things you need to look for when considering a DIY sound system or iPod wedding reception. Of course, I didn't touch on any of the actual "talent" required to run the event; I've covered those in previous chapters. As amazing a piece of equipment as an iPod is, one feature they can't build in is talent and experience.

Part II

Learn from 18 Top DJ Entertainers
from Different Parts of the Country and
Around the World

You Don't Need a DJ, You Need a Superhero!

Mark Brenneisen
CSGI Events

Do you want to look at pictures and videos years after your wedding and remember the great times you had with your family and friends? To do this, you need to have an entertainer who has a backup plan for everything and an out-of-the-box attitude. For your memories to be enjoyable and not regrettable, you need to sign with an entertainer who is regionally or nationally recognized for their professionalism. Where can you find such an entertainer? You're on the right page! My name is Mark Brenneisen, and I am the president of CSGI Events, which is located in Glens Falls, New York. Whether it is your wedding or any other event, big or small, you can expect a paramount experience when you hire us!

Everyone at CSGI Events shares one common belief: to create as many signature moments during a reception as possible. Let's face it, there are a lot of DJs out there who do the basics: play music and make people dance. A DJ or wedding reception entertainment director, as we like to call ourselves, at the next level recognizes that you only get one chance to capture emotions, get pictures that are just right, and to create signature moments. Top-level entertainers work with photographers and videographers to create and capture these moments. They instinctively get people together for group shots, surround the dance floor with guests for first dances, and involve more people during your special dances and traditional wedding events, thus ensuring these special moments are signature, becoming long-lasting memories for you and your spouse.

At the end of the day, the only thing that you get to keep and cherish, aside from a dress that ends up in a box, a cake that takes up space in the back of the freezer, and dried-up flowers, are pictures and videos of you and your guests. A top-level entertainer will ensure these pictures and videos are of you and your guests having an absolute blast. We, at CSGI Events, take our responsibility very seriously. We get one chance to get signature moments just right, so we make the most of each and every opportunity.

In addition to creating signature moments, we'll suggest changing up the traditional wedding order of events, thus making your reception unique and memorable. For example, switching the first dances to after dinner with candles, scheduling mini dance sets after the announcements before dinner, and telling love stories all create matchless, romantic, and, most of all, fun receptions! This type of ingenuity sets us apart from other DJ companies.

Becoming a premiere DJ company in upstate New York didn't

happen overnight. It has taken a lot of hard work and dedication to our craft to get us where we are today. DJing started off as a hobby of mine that quickly turned into spinning at nightclubs. Ten years of DJing at nightclubs with the occasional party or wedding was great, initially. After regularly attending seminars and conventions to hone my craft, a passion started to develop. In a single year, I worked over 100 weddings! Soon CSGI Events was born, and it has been a full-time, multi-operational system like none other in our region for a number of years. By providing a DJ and MC at all wedding receptions, we take the energy, interaction, and passion to a whole new level. As a result of ongoing training and seminars, my employees show their passion at every event. Our company regularly receives praise from our clients, stating that we are the DJs that brides dream of. They say this because we genuinely care about our clients, and that makes the reception noticeably special. The differences that set us apart from other run-of-the mill DJ companies are a result of passion, and it's awesome!

There are so many rewards that come from being passionate about your job. The personal rewards extend to my clients as well. Because we are passionate, CSGI Events is always looking for new and innovative ways to make your event unique and unforgettable. We actually came up with a game that won us the 2011 "Best New Game Award" at the DJ Times Convention in New Jersey. Every year, there is a competition for this title, and that year our company decided to sign up. We ended up being selected as one of the 12 finalists for the competition, and we eventually ended up winning the category we entered! What got our team through that competition was PMA—positive mental attitude! I attribute my PMA to my long-time friend and mentor, Mike Walter, who owns Elite

Entertainment in New Jersey. Simply stated, our team's positivity and creativity made the judges like us, which in turn made us win! We bring this same positivity and creativity to all of our events and weddings. Your wedding will be the best ever, the happiest day of your lives. You win! Hands down! Period.

There is only one type of wedding with our company, and that is a successful one. As a DJ, it is important to have a positive mental attitude with everything you do. I always say, "If you wake up and you're breathing, it's going to be a great day." I live by that. No matter how bad or sad things are, you're alive, you're breathing, and I am going to make your wedding successful. Done. This outlook comes mostly from my great friend and mentor, DJ Sean "Big Daddy" McKee, from Connecticut. I love him for all he has inspired in me, and continues to inspire each day I am alive.

On more occasions than I'd like to remember, I have been called on the day of a wedding and asked to DJ the reception because the other DJ company that was booked canceled at the last minute. During tragedies like this, our PMA prevails. A DJ bailing is obviously a high-stress situation for the bride, groom, and their families! Although I don't show it, this is a high-stress time for me, as well. But, with some simple setups, a quick briefing about the reception, and most importantly, a PMA, the once potentially disastrous wedding goes off without any further problems. Truth be told, we probably save about 12 events like this a year. Whenever and wherever a DJ is needed, we are the ones to save the day in our area.

To ensure our clients are never in a no-show DJ-type situation, we never fully book our DJs. We always keep them open for that specific reason—to *save* another event. This attitude was engrained in me when I served in the U.S. Coast Guard for four years, starting at 18 years of age. The Coast Guard motto is *Semper Paratus*, which translates to "always ready." I live by that philosophy in my career, as we at CSGI Events are always ready. Also, having a degree in criminal justice, and serving as an EMT and fireman for most of my life, I have always had to be prepared for anything and everything. This assurance gives great peace of mind to our clients, as they know they are in good hands with us.

At CSGI Events, we are professional, reputable, and insured. These aspects of a business are something that you must find in all of your vendors for the reception! When it comes to providing the entertainment for your wedding, don't rely on a friend or a family member to help you. As I mentioned before, I cannot tell you how many times a year that our office gets a call from a client who says that their DJ backed out for some reason or another. "Who are these DJs that constantly back out?" you may wonder. Well, you may be surprised to learn that it is often a very close friend or even a family member! Unfortunately, when you use friends or family, there are no contracts involved, and many times, people have no idea what will transpire at their own reception. After all, there is a reason why many judges advise not doing business with family. Don't learn the hard way. Remember these simple words: "Exceptional talent is not cheap...cheap talent is not exceptional." Eighty percent of the success of your reception will be a result of the entertainment you choose.

Luckily, there is a foolproof way to determine if your vendor is legit. If a DJ or other vendor is winning awards, or is in the spotlight regionally or nationally, there's probably a good reason for that. Industry recognition means that they are trying their hardest to achieve professional development goals, and not just going through the motions each week to make a quick buck. It is important to use vendors that belong to trade associations, chambers of commerce, or are speakers or educators in their fields.

Our company has a multitude of awards and professional memberships for two reasons. First, we accept that we can only get better by learning from others and developing our ideas to share with you. Second, professional memberships and certifications show our dedication to our continuing education, and desire to improve. Don't think twice about it: use professional, insured, and reputable vendors.

When hiring a professional, legitimate company like CSGI Events, creativity, passion, and talent will make your wedding day successful. You probably noticed a lot of weddings are exactly the same. You have probably been to some plain vanilla, boring weddings, and your guests have, too. Everyone knows how the order of the night is going to go. First, the ceremony, then a cocktail hour followed by introductions, first dances, special dances, toasts and blessing, the dinner hour, maybe some more formalities, and then the DJ is going to play a bunch of classics to get people on the dance floor. This boring format is the reason why people leave weddings early. Fortunately, this doesn't have to be the case. Good DJs change up the traditional schedule or at least make it more creative. When you work with us, we advise you how to do something fun and different for your guests! When you do, there is a good chance that they will remember your special day and not be in a hurry to leave it.

Again, hire vendors that are reliable, trustworthy, and creative because they will make your reception that much more memorable. Another tip to keep in mind is to give your DJ some breathing room when it comes to song selections. The night will be immensely more fun for you and your guests if you let the DJ read the crowd and not your playlist. Now, while we do allow our clients to pick

100% of the music for the reception, we find that those who do often let us play guests' requests halfway through the night. Sadly, when our clients insist on picking 100% of the music, they soon realize their error because they are the only ones on the dance floor

By allowing your entertainer to be flexible, he or she can elicit an energetic and powerful dance floor that satisfies all of your guests' musical tastes. There can always be a "do not play" list as well!

The final tip may seem obvious, but it is often overlooked. Select a venue where the bar area is in the same room as the space you rented. A lot of people don't think about it, but it can be catastrophic if the bar is located in an area separate from where the action will be happening. People will leave the action to go to the bar if it is too hot in the main room. Obviously, this departure decreases the number of people in the room, which means there are fewer people around you to share in your special day. If the bar is in the same room, people can see the fun everyone else is having. It's a simple detail, but it keeps everyone more involved and creates a celebratory environment for the duration of your reception.

So, if you are looking for an unforgettable night that you can look back on and re-live for many years to come, then look no further. With our efficient event planning process, unique sense of style, foolproof backup plans, and acute attention to detail, you will get the best night of your life when you sign with CSGI Events. It is definitely worth checking us out and setting up a get-to-know-you meeting. You will like everything we have to offer and won't regret your choice to go with a premium DJ service in upstate New York. We look forward to hearing from you soon!

About Mark Brenneisen

Mark Brenneisen is Upstate New York's leading wedding and special event entertainment director. His 20 years of experience includes over 1000 events and countless hours planning, directing, and executing flawless, successful special occasions for his clients. The secret to his success is his passion for his craft: unparalleled, unprecedented, and trendsetting passion that allows your wedding to be the best it can be!

A proud U.S. Coast Guard veteran, previous public safety officer, and fireman/E.M.T., Mark brings his discipline and organizational skills to your event, ensuring a most memorable experience for you and your guests.

Mark is the founder of CSGI Events, The Adirondack Wedding Association, and the Adirondack-Albany Chapter of American Disc Jockey Association. His clients get to share his creativity, ideas, and knowledge that come from many years of experience, industry training seminars, and conferences. Mark is the authority in his region for the most memorable receptions, all based on his philosophy: "One chance...to get the picture, to capture the emotion, and to create a signature moment."

His accolades include:

DJ Times Magazine's annual convention, seminar presenter 2009, 2010, and 2012.
DJ Times Magazine's annual convention, DJ of the year competition, "Best New Game," 2011
Wedding Wire "Brides' Choice" awards, 2012
Post Star newspaper Best of the Region Award, Disc Jockeys, 2010, 2011, and 2012
American Disc Jockey Association member, 2009-present

Contact the Adirondack Region's most sought after DJ/Emcee for your event!

Mark Brenneisen
518–792–6092
greg@csgievents.com
www.markbrenneisen.com / www.csgievents.com

Why a Top-Notch DJ Does Not Specialize in Music

Guy Artis
OHS Entertainment

Are you searching for a reputable, true professional to handle your wedding reception? Your wait is over! My name is Guy Artis, the owner of OHS Entertainment, located in Wilmington, Delaware. We provide top-notch customer service to our customers. What does this mean to you? It means that you are guaranteed a level of professionalism that will put your mind at ease on one of the most important and memorable days of your life! When you book our services, we make sure that your special day goes as seamlessly as possible. There are multiple wedding entertainers linked with OHS Entertainment, and we ensure that all of them are capable of approaching your wedding reception with the

highest regard. When you decide to do business with us, you can feel confident that you are getting one of the best entertainment services in the industry. It is the mission of OHS Entertainment to create everlasting memories for our customers.

My love for spinning records, better known as DJing, began in the early eighties during my high school years. A friend of mine owned a pair of turntables, and he would perform at the local house parties. I was his roadie, helping to carry his equipment and vinyl records. As a roadie, I would help him with house parties and other events in the neighborhood. One day, I attempted to spin on his turntables, and I discovered that I was good at this. Actually, I was GREAT at it! My passion for entertaining grew during the height of the hip hop era, when the art form of DJing was popular with Philly DJs such as Jazzy Jeff, Grandwizard Rasheen, Cash Money, Grandmaster Nell, and other local DJs, as they were at the height of their careers. My interest exploded from there. My passion for entertaining has led me to where I am today. When it comes to entertaining, I have always known that the ultimate goal is to make the people (customers) happy. When they are happy, I have done a great job!

Over the years, OHS Entertainment has built a solid reputation with many facilities in the Tri-State area. We offer professionalism that creates a level of trust with our customers, removing any doubt or anxiety prior to your special day. For example, one of our wedding customer contacted me regarding a potential problem. Her wedding reception was a few weeks away, and she disclosed to me that her pianist had cancelled on her at the last moment. As you can imagine, she was very upset and had no idea what she was going to do at this late date. I'm sure you can understand the stress this was causing her. My immediate thought was, "What can I do to help this customer?" Within one hour, I was able to provide her with the contact information for five pianists for her to interview. Do you see where I'm going with this? There is a lot to be said about customer service. It is all about serving the customers to the best of your ability. It did not take a lot of work to provide her with assistance. It relieved her stress, and for that, she was eternally grateful. In the end, the couple enjoyed our services, and was all-too-happy to sing our praises. Her response was: "OHS Entertainment is the BEST."

I am going to switch gears and talk about the "music" part of the business. Music goes hand in hand with customer satisfaction. Music selections are very important for you to talk about with your wedding entertainer. It is crucial that your wedding entertainer listens to you first, and understand the kind of atmosphere you would like to create at your reception. Only after listening to your wants

and needs should a wedding entertainer go by his or her professional judgment, and tell you what works and what does not. There are some customers that have very specific tastes in music. I try to let them know that even though they may like a certain style of music, there are so many age ranges to take into consideration while performing at a wedding reception. It is always good to have a diverse blend of music. You want to be able to work with guests' requests to make sure that they are having a good time. Appealing to diverse musical tastes is a rollercoaster ride. Please trust our judgment. However, we will take your input into consideration and incorporate it into your wedding reception.

Unfortunately, the type of customer service that I described is not in the protocol for some entertainment companies. For instance, a few years prior to staring OHS Entertainment, I worked for an entertainment company as one of their wedding entertainers. Some of the things that I witnessed were less-than professional. I knew that I could offer a much superior service than what I was seeing in the marketplace. You know the adage: people don't care how much you know; they want to know how much you care. As a result of much thought, I came to an easy decision to start my own entertainment company. Running an entertainment company, I have learned and listened to what is important to customers. I have also been able to offer sound advice where needed. Later on in the chapter, I will share with you some Q&A dialogue that will prove to be very helpful in your selection of an entertainment company for your wedding reception.

OHS Entertainment stands on its record that we provide top-notch services for our clients. Because of this, our customers are happy to give positive testimonials on our behalf!

Remember, hiring a true professional that you actually trust for your special day will ensure that you have a successful reception. First and foremost, OHS Entertainment is a customer-service driven company, and we do everything we can for our customers in regards to entertainment. Your only job is to relish the day. You did all the work up front, now it is time for you to enjoy it! So just relax (as much as you can) and have a good time because it's going to go like a blur. As long as you don't try to micromanage your wedding reception (because that's not your stress to carry, it's mine) and just enjoy the day, you will have a great time.

But I get it. For some of you out there, it is hard to sit back, relax, and enjoy everything. You just need to make sure that everything is going as you envisioned. That attitude is normally okay in life, but not for your special day! My desire is that you and your new spouse enjoy the day with your friends and family. At OHS Entertainment, we are committed to building your confidence in us during consultative meetings. We want you to be confident that you have hired the best company for your wedding. You will rest easy knowing that you hired an entertainment company that will follow through on your wishes. Often, after I have performed an event, I gain new friendships because of our superior service and showing that we care.

Now for the burning question that most prospective customers wants to know: "How much does it cost?" OHS Entertainment offers different packages to accommodate your needs. We are a market-oriented company, and our pricing is competitive. We offer professionalism and do it at a price that won't leave you with regrets. You can't beat that deal! If working with a company that is built on genuine customer service and endorsed by local facilities, then OHS Entertainment is for you!

About Guy Artis

Guy Artis is your "Premier Professional Party Entertainer." He has over 20 years of experience as a mobile disc jockey entertainer, performing for thousands of people within the Tri-State area of Philadelphia, Delaware, and South Jersey. His clients include ACME Markets, State of Delaware Division of Volunteerism, Hill International, NAES Corporation, and many private clients, just to name a few.

Guy is your "go-to-guy" for corporate and private events, if you are looking to have a successful, fun- filled, and stress-free event. He uses his knowledge and experience to create the atmosphere to fit the event of your desire.

Guy's customers enjoy more free time and autonomy by letting him design and program their event, ensuring a high rate of success for the customer and their guests. Guy is a certified member of N.A.M.E. (Name Association of Mobile Entertainers), and he is a co-founder of D.A.M.E. (Delaware Association of Mobile Entertainers). To learn more, contact us at the number below. We look forward to planning your special event with you!

Guy Artis
OHS Entertainment
888–433–1957
302–463–1937
www.ohsentertainment.com
www.facebook.com/ohsentertainment
www.twitter.com/ohsent

Give Your Reception the Winning Edge

Raymond Williams
Ebony Connections

Are you searching for quality entertainment for your wedding reception that will cater to your unique needs? Continue reading, now! My name is Raymond Williams, and I own Ebony Connections, located in Middle Island, New York. When we have our first interview, you'll see that I want you to feel like family. The last thing I want you to feel is stressed or pressured. The only thing that I stress is having professional quality entertainment at your reception. I'm so proud of my work, and because I stand by it, I show potential clients unedited footage from past events, so they can see exactly what they're going to get with me— everybody having a great time!

Building a company that consistently showcases quality entertainment isn't something that can be thrown together in a couple of hours. On your wedding day, I will be prepared for anything and everything that could happen. When preparing for your special day, I leave no stone unturned. For instance, I back up all of your song selections. All of your requests will be put in an iPod, or on a CD, external drive, or other backup device. The night before the event, I make sure that my van is packed with all the appropriate equipment—lights, party favors, and giveaways. I make sure my gas tank

> "I offer unique and different ways to make your wedding the one of your dreams."

is full and my clothes are packed. When I'm at the event, just before starting to perform, I have all the music ready for the intros. If I'm MCing, I meet the bridal party outside; I confirm everyone's name as I phonetically write out how to pronounce them, so I don't make any mistakes. I also like to place a name with a face, so that by halfway through the reception, I'm no longer needing that paper. I can look at their faces and remember who everyone is. This makes my clients and their guests feel very special. It's just one of the many little things I do that keep getting me rave reviews and future clients.

Becoming the owner of a reputable DJ business definitely took some hard work and concentration. While DJing, I used to also promote my own events, ski trips, boat rides, and dances. I eventually combined the two. Being both a promoter and a DJ, I was respon sible for all of the legwork: party planning, promoting of the event, renting the hall, and being the musical force. As you can imagine, that got to very tiresome. The market quickly became saturated with many new promoters, so I simply took out the promoting and planning part of my job and started offering my DJ services to people and other promoters. So, instead of me doing everything, I was hired exclusively to play at other people's events. Having had experience of preparing and coordinating an entire show allows me to offer you my perspective and advice as you find yourself in the difficult planning stages of your wedding.

Although I can do it all, I love focusing on being a DJ because of the adrenaline rush it gives me. I love getting people to party and have a good time. I have a lot of fun selecting music and taking the crowd on a musical journey. Before my event-promoting days, I started DJing as a teenager and fell in love with hip-hop. I later branched out to all genres of music, but I love seeing people enjoying themselves on the dance floor even more.

Now that I have my own DJ business, I offer unique and different ways to make your wedding the one of your dreams. For instance, one of the things that my company offers that not many DJ companies do is a bridal party bio. We compose and share a little biography about each bridal party member as they come into the reception hall during the introductions. With this, right out of the gate, your wedding reception is unique. I particularly like the bridal party bio because it adds some fun and flavor to the introductions and helps to set the tone for the party. Couples enjoy it because it lets their guests know who the people in the bridal party are and why they were chosen to be included in such a special way. Of course, the bridal party feels special because they are receiving an honor and recognition. With the bridal party bio, the guests quickly learn just who these special people are in a very entertaining way.

Unfortunately, unique and fun ideas don't come standard with all DJs. I do it because I really enjoy making people have a great time. Like I said before, with permission from my clients, I video-tape my events so that I can have footage to show potential clients. As a courtesy to the client whose event I taped, I send them a copy. With one client, when I sent them their copy, the bride confessed to crying because it had her father's toast on there, an event which no one else had captured. She called me to thank me over and over again. Because of this little thing that I did without even giving it a second thought, her father's speech was archived on film and audio so she could hear and see it over and over again. Having stories like this to reflect on make the little things I do to make your day extra special worth it!

Unlike other DJs, I don't rely on tricky marketing gimmicks to get business. Because I do a great job, referrals are the lifeline of my business. I am hoping that when I sit down with you for the first time, my presentation connects with you enough to hire me. Because I regard my clients as family, I don't want to trick you; I want you to choose me on the quality of work alone. After clients use our service, 99% of them are so satisfied that they willingly refer neighbors, family, and friends. I leave a lasting impression so that when you need a DJ, you'll think of me. I'm known as the guy with sensational service and fair pricing.

On occasion, not everything works out to perfection with wed-dings. However, a great DJ will make due, fix others' mistakes, and really try for the best. For instance, a couple of years ago a caterer didn't prepare enough food for the guests, so they ended up running out of food. People actually had to go to the nearby fast food restaurant to get food! To take attention away from this oversight, we played games and kept the music upbeat while people tried to take their minds off of what just happened. After people finished eating, the party started to die down. We knew just what to play, so we were able to turn the party up. We pumped up the party so much that everyone forgot about the food fiasco and just had fun. Long story short, that reception was the best party of the year.

Making a crowd completely forget about a huge oversight at a reception doesn't come without practice. To be completely honest with you, it is just something I developed by going out and hearing other DJs at other venues and events. However, using music to influence mood is a very important skill because once I get a crowd in a place where they are on the dance floor for hours, I can play any music you'd like to hear—any genre, any flavor. I can mix it and mash it up however you'd like. Your DJ must know your crowd. Unfortunately, your DJ will not know your guests in advance, so they only have that three- to four-hour window to figure out what they are into. Because of this, he or she should have asked questions about the ages and interests of people attending your event. This will help him or her determine their music preferences. Also, your DJ must ask questions about your personal musical selections, so that you can hear and dance to songs that you like.

Another tip that will make your reception fun and memorable is making sure to invite people who like to dance and have a good time. The attitude and mood of your guests will have a direct impact on your party and dance floor. If you're inviting people who don't normally dance, they're not going to start dancing at your wedding reception. So, it is important to know who you're inviting. Try to have an equal balance of males to females. Oftentimes, there can be a lot of single women and not enough men to dance with them, so it creates an imbalance. You will have tables of bored and lonely single ladies; they want men to dance with! So, it is very important to invite a good balance of people who like to have fun and dance.

Another tip to make your reception successful is thinking outside of the box. You and your guests probably have been to a lot of weddings, so think outside of the box so that your reception is different and memorable. I always ask my clients, "What is your vision for your reception, what you would like to see?" By their response, I can tell what kind of couple they are and offer suggestions to make their day unique to them!

Additionally, be a couple that likes to have fun and enjoy yourselves. It is important to find time to get on the dance floor and party. Have fun and let the DJ do the work. Don't place restrictions on your entertainment. Trust me, your reception will be a lot more fun. It is really cool when clients tell me that they have heard about my services through their family and/or friends, and they are completely confident in what I can do for them, so they let me take the reins. You already have enough things to worry about on that day; your DJ should not be one of them. After all, you hired a DJ to play music and to make sure that everyone has a good time at your reception, so let them do it!

Being too controlling can sabotage your wedding reception. Some clients that I have worked with in the past didn't allow the entertainers do what they do best. It is definitely okay to have your vision of how you see your wedding, but you are hiring entertainment for a reason: for us to entertain everyone, not just you! We have been doing this long enough where we can create an atmosphere for almost any type of reception you want. I have worked with couples that have a specific playlist, but their songs aren't the best party songs to get their guests up to dance and celebrate. We are professionals, so we know exactly what we are talking about when we tell you that a certain song may not give you the result you are looking for. As a DJ company that is here for you, we want to make sure that we play your requests while giving your guests some of the best wedding favorites to keep the dance floor packed.

It is absolutely critical that you understand time management at your wedding. The entire day is going to fly by as quickly as it came, so make sure that you take care of certain things before the dancing portion of the night begins. For instance, instead of taking your family out for pictures in the middle of a party set, take pictures before the wedding ceremony, or before the reception. When you leave to take family pictures in the middle of the reception, it kills the mood and dance floor, as it makes many of your guests feel left out. At Ebony Connections, we are always trying to move the protocol along at a good pace because we know that time is of the essence. You've got to eat your meal, greet your guests, cut your cake, and take lots of pictures. Make sure that you are aware of the time and know what things you have time for and what things you do not. You do not have all day to stretch things out, so manage your time wisely

Finally, the best advice I can give you when looking for a DJ is to be very cautious of going cheap on entertainment. It's nice to get a low or cheap price on some things, but with something as special as your wedding, that could be a very costly error in judgment. Remember, you can't get this night back! There are no DO OVERS! A DJ could have all the music in the world, but if they don't know how to put two beats together, or when to play the right music, what good does having all that music do? Make sure your DJ is more interested in you rather than their personal music collection! Do your research, read reviews. Read testimonials of different companies to see which one you may like best.

All in all, Ebony Connections is a great company that will not only take care of your wedding reception needs, but uniquely cater to them and give you a wedding reception that is out of this world. With our skills to read your crowd, and to play the right song at the right moment, you can be confident in knowing that your dance floor will be packed all night long. Enjoy yourselves and let us take care of the rest! I absolutely look forward to talking with you shortly!

About Raymond Williams

Ebony Connections was founded in 1990 as a party promotion company based out of Queens, New York.

By consistently providing quality music and professional services, the name "Ebony Connections" has become synonymous with "great parties." With our experienced DJs and energetic MCs, your wedding reception will be a non-stop party from the beginning to the end. We create unique packages to make your reception memorable beyond your wildest expectations.

At Ebony Connections, it is our goal to satisfy you, not as a one-time customer, but as a lifetime client. From your wedding day to your child's wedding day, and every special occasion in between, we want to be the ONLY choice you make for DJ entertainment. Let Ebony Connections be the key component to the success of your next event. With a list of satisfied clients too long to mention, references are available upon request. Give us a call to set up an entertainment evaluation and let us show you how we can meet your needs.

Raymond K. Williams
Ebony Connections Inc.
631–696–8383
info@ebonyconnections.net
www.ebonyconnections.net
www.ebonyconnections.com

Get Your Money's Worth, Or Get Your Money Back!

Kenya Conway
2Fyne Entertainment

Are you looking to go a different route for your entertainment on your special day? Well, look no further—your entertainment has arrived! My name is Kenya Conway, and I am the owner of 2Fyne Entertainment, located in Ellicott City, Maryland. One of the things that sets us apart from the traditional DJ company is that we have a team full of talented and highly skilled female DJs. That's right—the women are taking over. What used to be, and still is (for the most part) a male-dominated industry is becoming a little more used to seeing female faces behind the turntables and on the microphones. It is so fun to see the reaction of people when they find out that their DJ is a woman. 2Fyne

Entertainment is unique because we bring the female perspective, experience, and natural ability to "handle things" to the table.

Not only are we extraordinary party planners, we are extraordinary performers as well. Think about it: When you were growing up, who did most people go to when they wanted something done? The lady of the house, that's right! Well, this is no different, and no disrespect to my guys, but a woman's natural ability to connect with people and get the job done, without leaving any stones unturned, is like no other. As a business owner, I feel the most important thing is educating my clients, making sure that they are aware of all of the options that are available to them, pros and cons in different scenarios, and then, of course, helping the clients' dream event become a reality. It's okay with me, however, if someone decides to use another DJ company. I believe in abundance, so in my mind, there is no shortage of business. I have a similar mindset when working with clients, as well: "While someone else is making excuses as to why something can't be done, I'll show you 10 ways it CAN be done."

I was a former school teacher, and I loved it; it was very rewarding. I was able to really connect with my students and relate to them on so many levels. They thought it was awesome that their teacher was a DJ. Oftentimes, I would play music for my classes while they were working; it was the coolest thing for them. I also would bring in equipment on special days and teach them about what I had and let them play with it. Eventually, I started offering DJ lessons through the Howard County Recreation & Parks Program, where students from all across the county participated. What a great time! So not only was I DJing events, I was also giving lessons. My business started to grow, and I began to see that I could really do something big in this industry. So I combined my love of music and entertaining and created 2Fyne Entertainment.

At 2Fyne Entertainment, we are not a run-of-the-mill DJ Company. It's funny. When clients initially call us, the first question they ask is usually, "How much do you charge?" Unfortunately, we cannot immediately put a price on what we do. We educate our clients and customize every detail specific to their event. It's an experience that we create, not just music. We virtually plan every detail of your event and work with your other vendors to ensure a seamless and stress-free experience for you. You can choose from our beautiful lighting packages that will add elegance and sophistication, as well as custom monograms that can be projected throughout the room. Another fun experience we offer is "Dancing in the Clouds," which looks amazing in pictures. The couple dances in a foggy haze that appears as if they're dancing on clouds. "Love Stories" are a great way to kick off your reception just before the grand entrance of the bridal party; it's sure to be something that your guests will never forget. (When we get together, I will reveal what Love Stories are, plus more special touches that you will only see with 2Fyne Entertainment).

I take the work of my company so seriously and stand behind it with the utmost confidence, that I offer a 100% money back guarantee for all of my events. You can absolutely be sure that you will get your money's worth plus some. I decided to put this policy in place to show that I am dedicated to the success of my clients' event and will put as much time, effort, and energy into the preparation and performance.

People have described me as being very personable and a pleasure to work with. My people skills came in handy one evening during a reception when the bride and groom got into a tiff with each other. It was very obvious that they were fighting and at each other's throats. That's when I stepped in and got the bride and the bridesmaids out on the dance floor for some good ole quality girl time. This took the bride's mind off of whatever was going on and got her smiling and having fun again. When the other guests saw how much fun we were having, they came out and joined us—and so did the grumpy groom. We danced our hearts out, and the bride was very thankful that I recognized the problem and stepped in to help. The excitement and energy helped the couple to forget about their problems, and from that point on, the night was drama-free, and everyone had a great time. Only an expert can do that.

If I had to give couples advice for the evening of their reception, the first thing I would recommend is to be sure to hire a professional DJ. So often, couples try to cut costs; however the DJ is the most important part of the reception, so that is not an area that you want to skimp on. Don't hire your nephew the hobbyist or your friend from down the street who has a good stereo system. Your wedding is a once-in-a-lifetime event that will be one of the biggest purchases of your life, and you can't leave it to chance. There are so many things that could go wrong or throw a wrench in plans that only a professional will be equipped to handle. I can't stress enough how important the DJ's role is for your event. Your DJ will act as emcee, seeing to it that the timeline of the evening is moving smoothly and that all of the vendors are in sync and ready to move on to the next activity. Your DJ will make sure that the photographers/videographers are aware of what's coming next in order to be sure to capture your photographic memories. Everyone relies on the DJ to find out what's happening next on the itinerary. Additionally, your DJ will be the emcee and the entertainer extraordinaire. Please make sure your DJ feels comfortable with and is good on the microphone. There is nothing worse than hearing someone on the microphone with no speaking skills. They may can spin some music, but please don't ask them to talk. I've been hired just to come emcee events because the DJ didn't feel comfortable on the mic.

When choosing your DJ, make sure that he or she fits your personality and style. As a teacher, I learned very quickly how to work with different types of personalities in many different situations, so it's easy for me to adapt with whatever is called for. I have been known to get out on the dance floor with the guests, show new dance moves, and just plain have fun with them. I'm not shy about that. My energy and enthusiasm is contagious.

Choosing the music that will be played that evening is also very important. You want to make sure you allow your DJ to play a variety of songs that reach multiple generations. The worst thing you can do is play one type of music the entire night, not taking into consideration all of your guests. I've had brides who absolutely hate line dances, and I've had to honor not playing the line dance songs. But guess what? The same songs that the brides didn't want me to play were the very same songs that their guests were asking for. In that instance, I simply cleared it with the bride first, then played the requested music. Other advice is for the bride and groom to be active participants in the reception, basically meaning that when the bride and groom dances, everyone dances. Your guests are not going to leave you on the dance floor alone, so the more you participate, the more everyone else will participate.

Allow your DJ some flexibility. When you hire a professional, you are paying us to fill your dance floor, read the crowd and inter-

act with them, and choose songs that your guests can dance to and enjoy. It is helpful when the client gives us an idea as to the different genres that they like and even gives us some of their favorites, but don't hold so closely to a strict list. An experienced DJ will know what to play and when to play it.

There is so much power in music. I love it! Music can alter the way people feel in an instant, and the fact that I have control over that is exciting. With the proper mix of music, I can motivate and encourage people, make them want to dance, make love, relax, and even cry. Music is so powerful, and I love that I get to use it in a way that brings joy to my clients and make them feel good.

Timing is another important factor to consider when planning your event. Make sure you leave enough time for travel between venues, enough time for pictures, and enough time for a receiving line should you decide to have one. The worst thing you can do is to arrive late and cut into the reception time. You've spent all of this time and money planning for your dream day, be sure that you can enjoy every minute of it. Typically, receptions are four hours long, but maybe you should consider a five-hour reception just to be sure. It has been so disheartening to see couples lose out on dancing time because of starting late. I would always feel so bad. So... one way to help avoid this issue is to allow yourself enough time to get ready, for transportation, etc. Start on time!

There are other critical things to keep in mind when working with vendors. Do they have liability insurance? Do they have back-up equipment? What happens in the event of illness or inclement weather? Do they have a money-back guarantee or refund policy, and what do their references say? Don't leave your special day to chance. Protect yourself by working with reputable professionals

in the industry.

Finding the right vendors for your reception can turn an ordinary event into an extraordinary event because the synergy that is created when we work together is immeasurable. I believe in creating personal relationships and business partnerships with other vendors, and I am connected with an elite network of bridal professionals. If a client is having trouble finding quality vendors, no problem, I can connect them with some superior service professionals.

To sum it up, don't short change yourself on one of the biggest days of your life! Let 2Fyne Entertainment hold your hand every step of the way. We will reveal the secrets of having an amazing wedding. We look forward to serving you!

About Kenya Conway

Kenya Monique Conway, owner of 2Fyne Entertainment Professional DJ Service in Ellicott City, Maryland, began her journey in the entertainment industry many years ago as she pursued her love of music and desire to entertain. Making quite a name for herself, Kenya has performed at numerous weddings, promotional events, and other occasions all across the Maryland/DC/Virginia area. Some of Kenya's corporate clients in-clude Victoria's Secret, Macy's, Bloomingdale's, David's Bridal, B.E.T, Jackson and Tull, Raytheon, and Giant, just to name a few. A former teacher, Kenya has combined her love of teaching with her passion for entertaining by instructing a series of DJ classes for teenagers.

Kenya especially enjoys performing at weddings because each

event is different, varying in types of music, personalities, mood, and atmosphere. "I enjoy having the opportunity to take the bride and groom's vision of their perfect wedding and turn it into an amazing reality." Kenya's favorite part of the wedding reception is the introductions. "I absolutely love introducing the entire bridal party and the whole excitement and buildup that leads to announcing the bride and groom. The music is high energy; the guests are standing, clapping, and waiting with anticipation. What a fun time!"

When Kenya is not on the turntables, she is no slouch when it comes to entrepreneurship. She has become a highly sought after motivational speaker and teacher on topics pertaining to personal and corporate development. Kenya conducts powerful, life changing, and comprehensive training workshops to groups and individuals aspiring to improve their current results. Since reclaiming her first love of public speaking, coupled with her natural knack for teaching, Kenya has become a force to reckon with, as she inspires, motivates, and teaches audiences of all ages how to break the barriers that are keeping them from accomplishing their wildest dreams.

Kenya holds a Master's Degree in Curriculum & Instruction and Educational Leadership from McDaniel College in Westminster, Maryland. She has also been trained at the Scratch DJ Academy in New York, as well as the Beat Refinery in Bethesda, Maryland.

Kenya Conway
2Fyne Entertainment Professional DJ Service
443–398–1414
kenya@2fyneentertainment.com
www.2fyneentertainment.com

The Practice of Perfect Planning

Jimmie Esposito
Move It Music DJ and Lighting

Are you looking for a quality, highly regarded entertainer that has experience, personality, and poise to make your special day truly memorable while representing your style? Then, you've stopped at the right page in this book! My name is Jimmie Esposito; I am the founder of Move It Music DJ and Lighting, headquartered in Boston, Massachusetts. Move it Music is an award-winning, full service entertainment company that knows how to enhance your wedding day with the perfect music, professional lighting and attention to detail that will truly represent your style and personality. We have been producing unforgettable events throughout the Boston area since 1998.Our

An elegant dance party at the Hotel Viking Newport.
Photo credit: lisarigbyphotography.com

Last dance of the night at Crane Estate.
Photo credit: benoit-mccarthy.com

professional wedding DJ's play the perfect mix of music for your ceremony and reception and feature the latest in digital sound and lighting equipment to ensure that your special day will be one to remember. Our masters of ceremonies are consummate professionals and passionate about the success of your event.

Move It Music has a unique approach to Boston area wedding ceremonies and receptions. Our ability to help you create a consistent musical theme is what sets us apart from the rest. We interpret your wishes, and help to shape your special day with music, all while taking other ceremony and reception details such as color, style and sophistication into consideration. For example, when our brides and grooms incorporate unity sand into their ceremonies, we set this special moment to music to enhance the experience. It is undeniable, that music sets the tone of a wedding ceremony, cocktail hour and reception. A polished DJ ensures smooth transitions between these portions of your event while making memories through music.

Like I said before, our specialty lies in the details; we are not just DJ's. We will guide you through your special day leaving nothing to question. We are, in fact, helping to plan your entire event by asking the right questions and eliminating the margin for error in the planning process. To ensure a flawlessly executed event, no detail is overlooked. By orchestrating every detail according to our planning forms, we ensure moments like the cake cutting ceremony and parent dances will be timelessly displayed in your wedding album forever. We advise your guests who will be giving speeches, where to stand to ensure the perfect photos, how to speak into and hold the microphone, and we even help to calm down the Best Man if he is nervous.

The orchestration of your wedding formalities is an important part of what makes Move It Music a unique entertainment company. Our music and timing represents our couples in a manner which always keeps in mind the overall event. What most wedding guests will remember is the fun factor! Our goal is to keep the dance floor packed at all times, this can be a challenge with small crowds. Our DJ's are actually "real DJ's" mixing and remixing music on site to keep your guests excited the entire evening. We have a talent for mixing together just the right combination of classics and new tracks to create a vibe that you just can't resist. When it all comes down to it, your Wedding is the one of the biggest days of your life! It is an honor for us to be a part of such an amazing celebration; and also a huge responsibility. The DJ and MC create the vibe for the entire evening, and can either make or break your wedding. We feel that because we incorporate design, planning and execution into every wedding, that we are ensuring the success of your special day.

For instance, just this past October I had the pleasure of personally working with this beautiful couple from Boston. They were so excited to be getting married and really looking forward to the perfect evening. When I met with them, they indicated that it was imperative that I meet with the bride's parents before committing. This meeting went very well, and I felt an immediate connection to the family — the couple booked the very next day.

During the planning process, the bride had some concerns about her dad. He was going through cancer treatments, and was very tired and a little unsure on his feet. She really wanted to dance with him at her wedding, but also wanted him to be able to maintain his pride in front of his friends and family. So, working together, we revised the timeline and formalities so they could have this very special dance very early in the evening, before her dad was too tired

Rocking the dance floor at The Commons 1854.
Photo credit: benoit-mccarthy.com

In the Mix at Spinelli's Lynnfield.
Photo credit: bostonweddingphotos.com

from all of the festivities. Turns out the dance went great and he was on the dance floor a little bit later that night, really enjoying the fun!

Fast forward two months — I get a phone call from the bride to thank me for everything that we did for her and her family; and to let me know that her dad had passed away just that week. She needed to let me know because her dad made it a point to tell her that her wedding was the absolute best day of his life, and he had never been so proud. He had so much fun, and attributed this to how we were able to make him and everyone else at the reception feel special because no detail was over looked.

This is an example of why I and our DJ's here at Move It Music work as wedding DJs. We truly are blessed to have such a positive impact on so many lives!

So, if like this bride, you want to have a successful wedding that people will still be talking about for years to come, there are a few things that you should do to ensure this success. Don't worry; we will help you along the way. I look at a successful event as one that goes according to plan. Move It Music's detailed timelines and completed event forms are the ultimate key to your wedding's success. More and more couples are allowing their hired professionals to help put a plan together for the evening.

During the initial meeting, we get to meet you, discuss what we can do for you, and our advantages over the other entertainment companies. We also take some time to understand and get to know you, in order to make sure that we are a good fit for your wedding. We want to learn about where you grew up, what you do for work, your music tastes and what your friends and family are like. The more we can learn about you, the better we are able to produce the perfect wedding! We are selective about who we choose to

The DJ's got her fallin' in love at Spinelli's Lynnfield
Photo credit: bostonweddingphotos.com

Hands Up on the dance floor at The Commons 1854.
Photo credit: dandoke.com

work with because we think it's very important to fit the DJ with the bride and groom together perfectly. If we don't feel we will be a good fit, some thing with your style, your wants, your needs or if what you're looking for is something we can't provide, we want to know that right away because we want to master your wedding. We will never take on a wedding and try to wing it. We want to be able to give you the absolute best possible experience.

After that initial meeting, comes the decision making process. Taking into consideration how important the perfect DJ is to your wedding we want you to take your time with this decision. If you have read through all of our 5 Star Reviews, researched our references and are excited as we are to work together, then we would Love to be your wedding DJ!

Once booked, you will receive your login to our online portal and will begin filling out your planning forms. Leading up to your wedding date there is a six month planning meeting. At this meeting, we discuss how we will make your wedding unique from everyone else's. We also talk about essential wedding details like custom introductions for your bridal party and custom voiceovers for your parent dances that are just completely unlike anything your wedding guests have ever seen. We will discuss the level of DJ interaction with your crowd to get everybody dancing, with efforts to create great photos for the event. After this meeting, you will have everything you need to complete your online forms and timeline for the wedding day.

The most important logistical meeting is your final meeting. At this meeting, all of our plans are locked down, understood and agreed upon by all parties. We go over each and every detail, and finalize your timeline. We account for and discuss every aspect of

your ceremony and reception to ensure you will make the most out of every moment. Everyone leaves this meeting excited knowing that the event is going to be perfect; ensuring our clients truly enjoy their day by allowing the professional's to take over

An important tip for a successful night; if you really want all of your friends and family up and dancing...you both need to be on the dance floor as much as possible. Your guests will want to be with you all night, so they naturally gravitate towards the bride (yes, and groom as well). Everyone wants to have a great time and they want to do it with you!

A final tip to ensure that your wedding reception is very successful is to not put too many limitations on your DJ. When you hire a professional, he knows how to balance your tastes with that of the dancing crowd. On your wedding day, we never leave our turntables and there are no automated playlists. We will be choosing each song live and putting together a unique soundtrack for you and your guests. Weddings are a family event; true wedding DJ's understand this, and tailor the evening to keep all ages on the dance floor together. We encourage our clients to inform us of their favorite songs. We have a comprehensive interactive website that allows our brides and grooms to securely build their Must Play, Please Play and Do Not Play Lists. These lists are taken very seriously. The goal is to deliver the service that you want while taking the steps to educate you about different ways to keep all of your guests happy.

Now you have the information, but what are you going to do with it? Do you actually know how to pick a DJ that will be a good fit for you and your wedding guests? It is a lot harder than it first seems. There are many factors that you should consider when choosing your DJ. One important factor is the poise and the confidence of the DJ to know that he's an expert in the field. Also, the company's flexibility in giving each and every bride and groom exactly what they want for their wedding. Their level of detail should also come into consideration. Are they actually listening to you and helping to tailor the perfect evening around your vision?

The most important tool you have when considering the perfect DJ for your wedding is research. You should research the individual DJ and his company's reputation. How do they look online? Reference checking is very important to understand what the rest of the community thinks about this vendor. Their technology and sound equipment should also be considered. Most people don't really know much about sound systems or turntables, but it's very important to ask some basic questions. Do they have state of the art equipment? Are they updating their equipment regularly? Can they provide all of the necessary sound systems for separate locations for formalities or multi roomed venues? How does their equipment compare to others in the industry? Of course consider things like the appearance of both the DJ and his equipment at the wedding. What does the DJ provide in his package? How is their table dressed? How are their wires hidden? Your venue will be beautiful, the bride will look beautiful, but how will the DJ look? How does he make his system look clean to match with everything else?

Lastly, pricing and contract terms need to be discussed. In the Boston area, there are hundreds of DJ's in competition; and the pricing ranges everywhere from $500 to upwards of $4000 to provide your wedding entertainment. The cheap DJ's will try to tell you that the services provided between the high and low end DJ's are exactly the same. Trust your instinct and do your research, this is obviously not true. So, understanding where the market is and where the experience lies is also very important when choosing a DJ.

After everything is said and done, what everyone remembers from the wedding is if they had a great time. While all of the above mentioned factors are extremely important, the most important thing that you should look for is the connection that you feel during the interview process. Choosing the right professional DJ for your wedding is extremely important, and plays heavily into the success of the overall event. You are going to be working with us, your DJ, for the entire 12 to 18 months leading up to the wedding: discussing music details, coordinating introductions, planning the timeline, even designing lighting and decor. Building a great relationship is important, and will enable the DJ to carefully customize the event perfectly to compliment the bride and groom. Without the connection, the planning process is boring, unproductive and off target.

I know that this is a lot of information, and your wedding is one of the biggest days, of your life. This can be a stressful time because you want it to be as perfect as possible without any flaws. It is important to plan ahead and think about all of the things that I have talked about. However, when it comes down to it, the best piece of advice I can give you is to be confident. It doesn't matter what happens during the planning process, it doesn't matter what went wrong that morning or what family member is being difficult. Once you walk up there and get ready to start the ceremony and reception, confidence is your best accessory, and no one else will notice if anything's wrong. And remember, we always have your back.

Finally, while the wedding industry in New England is amazing; the real reason we do this job is because we LOVE it! It is an honor and privilege to play such an important role in helping to make your wedding day perfect. We receive countless letters and online posts from brides and grooms about how Move It Music "made" their wedding! Our clients rave about how we were perfect and how the night would not have happened without us! We truly have the BEST job in the world!

The information is all here. You have read the testimonials and reviews. Now it's your turn. What are you waiting for? Does an award-winning, full-service entertainment company sound like something that you want for your once-in-a-lifetime day? There's no reason for you not to have the best. We can't wait to meet you!

About Jimmie Espo

DJ Jimmie Espo, owner of Move It Music DJ and Lighting, has been a successful disc jockey for over 20 years; his versatile resume spans from performing at the hottest Boston nightclubs in the early to mid-90s to becoming the polished professional wedding Master of Ceremonies that you see today.

DJ Jimmie Espo entered into the wedding entertainment industry in 1998, where he brought his fresh approach at mixing old and new music, providing a packed dance floor for all ages. He opened Move It Music in the same year. Now, Jimmie performs at over 90 Weddings per year throughout New England and is recommended by the area's top wedding venues. He has been featured in many publications, including *Brides Magazine* and *Newport Bride,* as well as dozens of online platforms. In addition, Jimmie has co-authored the book *How to Plan the Perfect New England Wedding: Featuring 16 Interviews with New England's Top Wedding Professionals.* Move It Music DJ and Lighting has been awarded numerous "Bride's Choice Awards," and in 2012 was named *The Destination Guide's Best DJ Company in New England.*

DJ Jimmie Espo and Move It Music also help to create the perfect look for your wedding ceremony and reception with ultra-modern lighting effects and custom monograms. Jimmie Espo is the proud creator of the "air booth," a state-of-the-art, one-of-a-kind photo kiosk for weddings and special events.

Despite his widespread success, DJ Jimmie Espo has remained humble and eager to please his clients. He listens to the wishes of the bride and groom and executes accordingly. This is how he has established himself as one of the hottest wedding DJs in New England. To learn more, contact Move It Music today.

DJ Jimmie Espo
Move It Music DJ & Lighting
866–MOVEIT–1 / (866–668–3481)
espo@moveitmusic.com
www.moveitmusic.com
Facebook: facebook.com/moveitmusic

How to Have a Stress-free Event!

Javier Montes
Entertainment Management Group

Brides and grooms, if you are looking for a completely unique and customized experience for your wedding day, look no further. Hello, my name is Javier Montes, and I am the owner of Entertainment Management Group (also known as EMG, and formerly known as DJ Connection), located in Miami, Florida.

No two events at EMG are exactly the same. We build your event from the ground up and make it unique to you. With features such as custom lighting decor, online event planning tools, custom surround-sound-systems, and EMG event designers and lighting engineers that meet with you to understand your vision, you can see how EMG can make your event the one of your dreams!

It is very important to me that all of my employees, which I personally hire and train, are extremely professional and dedicated to EMG 100%. When you hire us, you get legitimate professionals who know what they're doing—not some subcontractor or young kid who just DJ for a hobby. Since our DJs are authentic, South Beach club-style mixers, we develop a unique vibe at each of our events. Your event needs to be taken seriously, and I personally strive to find those people who will do so. Finding quality entertainers is important to us because we have had some very high-profile clients, such as Queen Elizabeth of England, Adrienne Arsht, the British American Chamber of Commerce, the Spain Chamber of Commerce, American Express, University of Miami, South Florida politicians, and the list goes on.

Building EMG has been a fantastic experience for me. After spending years in corporate America, I decided to start working on my business. It started growing very rapidly, so I brought on one more person to work with me. I trained that person to work exactly like I work, because my clients loved my personal style and professionalism. I wanted to make sure that each of my clients was getting the same style, even though I was not personally performing at their event. Long story short, EMG has grown to be one of the largest entertainment companies in South Florida, and we are now international! Clients fly us all over the world on a regular basis to ensure that their event will "WOW!" their guests!

EMG strives for excellence, perfection, and flawless execution at every event, and my clients are extremely happy with the results. My clients can enjoy a stress-free and happy event. Not too many brides and grooms REALLY enjoy their wedding to the MAX! At the end of my clients' "Dream Wedding," they just have a smile from ear to ear and thank me. Because of this, I know I will be part of their memories for the rest of their lives. This is the best reward I can receive. I do not DJ to just "make a quick buck." I have a great passion for my business and my clients. I develop a close, genuine relationship with each one of my clients because I listen to and understand what THEY want. Every single client is different, and that's an exciting challenge for me. I am eager to go to work every single day, and my clients are thrilled to come see me. It's a fun job!

EMG has been very successful because all of the events we do are unique. What most clients don't realize is that 60 to 70% of our work is done prior to their event. We spend a lot of time identifying what you want and what you would like to see the day of your event. I don't want you stressed at your event, or managing the entertainment. I want you to experience and enjoy your event! Many couples spend a ton of time preparing an event—doing all kinds of stressful stuff. You see them the night of the event, and they are running around like chickens without their heads! With this pressure, they cannot enjoy the night. Instead, they are excited for it to be over with! This is a travesty, and it's why EMG spends so much time preparing before every event. You are my client. You are choosing me because I am a professional entertainer. My job is to worry about the details at the event. Let me and my team handle all the stress for you! Your job is to ENJOY the experience.

Our experience gives us an edge because we know ways to help your event go smoothly, and for it to be more fun and enjoyable for everyone. We do this by focusing on the little things. Little things matter! When we catch the bride and groom swamped in conversations with their guests, we'll surprise them with a cocktail or bottle of water. You are the stars of the night, and we want you to be taken care of.

Because customer service is such a valuable aspect of EMG, we make sure to schedule an event evaluation at our office with every single client BEFORE we do anything else. At this orientation, we will discuss your wedding dreams and ideas to make sure that we are all on the same page—that our style is going to match your style. We want to make sure from day one, that you understand the magic that we are going to provide for your special day. Most of our clients have come to us because they have seen what we have done for one of their friends, or they have been to one of our company parties, and they always comment on how EMG's style is so amazing and unique! We are not your typical "DJ." We are modern entertainers who will be upfront with you from day one!

We also make sure that you understand your responsibilities as a client. We are not the kind of company where you come in, sign the contract, and we say, "Good luck! I'll see you the day of the event!" We don't ask you to do a lot of hard work; all we ask for is information about the event and your particular vision, so we can plan and give you our expertise on the items that you may not have thought about, or that you may not have known even existed! Because our events are so customized to you, we need your input. Don't worry, we'll lead you through all the options and answer every question you have. You do not have to be alone planning this big day! Let our years of experience and attention to every detail shine through every minute of your event! Every stage of the planning process is critical, as it ensures a smooth transition into assembling the event that your guests will talk about for YEARS to come.

As a professional entertainer, I think my job is very important, and I take it very seriously. Most event professionals will tell you there are two main things that people are going to remember about your event: the food and the fun they had (or didn't have). So, take your time picking those things! Budget accordingly for food and entertainment because it will determine the success of your event.

It's important to stick with the professionals and get referrals when hiring for your event. There are a lot of horror stories out there about those who have tried to save a couple of dollars by not hiring the pros. I encountered one situation at an outdoor wedding where the bride, and the company she rented a tent from, were on different pages about how the event should go. She wanted the tent covered up with a curtain so that people would be surprised when they walked in after the cocktail hour was over. The people who rented her the tent were not only being rude to the bride on HER wedding day, but they told her that she didn't order a curtain and that it wasn't part of their contract. I happened to overhear the conversation, so I gently stepped in and told her that I would take care of it. After a quick call to my guys in our warehouse, a curtain was completely set up within an hour. Unfortunately, more problems arose for this poor bride because of her poor planning. She hired florists, not only to provide flowers, but to do the lighting as well. Nowadays, everyone thinks that they can do lighting! Once again, I could see she was unhappy with the results. In my opinion, the lighting was atrocious. So I stepped in, relocated the lights, programmed them properly, and we created the exact color lighting she wanted. A true professional not only spots problems, but fixes them as quickly and gracefully as possible.

This is one of the biggest days of your life, so why hire someone who entertains on the side? Why would you put your event in the hands of a friend or uncle who hasn't done a single event of this size in their lives? You certainly aren't going to ask your aunt to cater your wedding just because she enjoys baking on the weekends! We are full-time professionals. This is our job. Give me your ideas, and I will turn them into realities!

One of the first things that I tell all my couples is that it is very important for you to meet potential vendors in person and make sure you feel comfortable with them from day one. It is extremely important that you develop a connection with the vendors and feel they understand what your needs and wants are. If you don't do this, you risk your event becoming a complete disaster. Trust your gut! If you do not feel comfortable with a vendor from day one, if they are sub-par from the beginning, trust me, once you've given them a deposit, it is only going to get worse from there.

I understand price is important, and it's tempting to choose the cheaper vendor, but if you do not feel 100% comfortable with a person, it will most likely not end well. Always meet with people you hire in person. This is the best way to find out if they are a good fit for you. A person may sound professional on the phone or via email, but when he or she shows up with a huge pink Mohawk at a black tie formal tuxedo event, you probably will not be very happy. Please do not skimp on certain services just because of price. Make sure to go above and beyond, and definitely try to pick vendors that you are really, really comfortable with. Doing this will allow you to TRULY enjoy your special day!

Rely on professional advice! I work events every single week-end, so I know what I am talking about. Professional florists know what they are talking about and the same goes for professional photographers and videographers. Do not try to force things on vendors or restrict them from doing something other than what you want because you fear that the night will not go as smoothly as planned. Relax. If you invested the time into hiring a true professional, we should know what we are doing. You obviously selected a particular vendor because they are somebody that you trust, so please, listen to them. Trusting your vendors will make your reception successful and enjoyable! This will make the difference between being stressed at your event and enjoying it.

Here's an example of how micro managing your vendors can have a negative effect on your event. In the past, people came up to me before the reception began and said, "Here is a list of songs to play. Play them in this specific order!" Thankfully, this doesn't happen anymore because of the extensive planning we do before the party, but in those cases in the past, after playing the specified playlist, when no one was dancing to the music, they usually come up to me crying, "Please, play whatever you think is best because my wedding is a disaster!" Even the best-planned selection of music can sometimes fall flat. Don't worry! I know how to read a crowd and rock a party. I know how to change things up on the fly when the party needs an injection of energy. Whether the crowd is young, old, laid-back, or wild—I can get people to have one of the most AMAZING nights of their lives. You just tell me the road map of what you would like to see for your reception, and I will make it happen.

Here's a little tip from my years of experience: Start the dancing portion of the evening as quickly as possible. People can only sit in their seats for a couple of hours, at most, before they start to get restless and BORED of all the wedding formalities. Your guests want to have fun, so the faster you get them up out of their chairs and dancing, the faster they will begin making memories for years to come.

South Florida has an extremely diverse culture. There are all different types of backgrounds and ages, and it is further diversified because it is popular for destination weddings for couples from all over the world. "Hora Loca" which translates to "Crazy Hour" has become very popular, uniting the diversity of South Florida. Many of our weddings are choosing to have "Crazy Hour" now. At a predetermined point in the evening, we hand out whatever the client has chosen, whether it be glow products, Mardi Gras beads, or special types of masks. We set the music to a very upbeat type of percussion for energetic dancing, and can even create a custom Hora Loca Mix for your event! Some couples opt to have us bring out party dancers and even LIVE percussionists! It's a fun and different experience for every single one of your guests! We always want to make sure that our diverse clientele has the latest and greatest from all over the world. Whatever it is, we will bring it, or we will ship it here, so that you have the best and can blow your guests' minds!

What enhances the experience further is that our lighting is completely computerized. For example, you might want to light the room blue when your guests walk in, and then pink when you walk in. When you do your first dance, you can change the room to white and put spotlights on you during your first dance! With computerized lighting, you can have a completely programmed light show for your event, giving you complete freedom for everything you want to do. I always tell my clients, "If you can dream it, I can create it!" Try me!

EMG prides itself in setting new trends in the event industry. Companies from all over the world keep an eye on us to see what new products we are offering our clients. One of the hottest and most requested products that we just launched is the world's first touch screen DJ board. It's a very unique product, and we're the only company in South Florida to offer it. Imagine if a DJ would DJ ONLY from a giant piece of glass (kind of matrix style or Iron Man style). On this piece of glass, we'll drag and drop songs, and load them on to a virtual turntable. You can see a picture of this on our Facebook page (www.facebook.com/DiscoverEMG). The touch screen DJ board eliminates turntables and CD players, and the crowd gets to watch everything we're doing. You and your guests get to watch us mix and see the sound waves move across the board. Upon seeing this, people typically say, "Oh my God, is that real?" This is just another one of those special touches we have that is sure to impresses your guests, giving them an unforgettable experience!

At EMG, we make sure that everyone is enjoying themselves no matter what. For a truly unique, energetic, Miami, luxurious South Florida reception entertainment and lighting experience, look no further. I look forward to meeting you!

About Javier Montes

Javier Montes is a well-known, respected, and trusted name in the event entertainment industry. Javier has over 15 years of personal hands-on experience in social, corporate, and private affairs. His personal clients include Nestle, Colgate, American Express, Costco, Queen Elizabeth of England, Adrienne Arsht, and Norwegian

Cruise Line, just to name a few.

Javier enjoys working with creative clients who have a clear dream for their special event. He routinely seeks out clients who are willing to push the limit of what most others in his field are too scared to ever try to accomplish!

Besides events, Javier is also a professional MC, on-air radio host, celebrity brand ambassador, TV show host, and serves as an event host for various local charities. Being fluent in both English and Spanish has helped Javier bring his talents to different parts of the world.

Javier can be booked for national and international events. He LOVES to travel! To check his availability, please visit the website or call the number below. Javier will not secure reservations that are more than two years away. Discretion is exercised for celebrity events.

"The most rewarding feeling in the world is when a bride looks at me with a smile from ear to ear, because I just made all of her wedding dreams a complete reality! It's so incredibly AMAZING that I get to be such an important part of one of the most important days in someone's life."—Javier Montes

Javier Montes
305–261–3550
888–9PROS–DJS
contact@thedjconnectioninc.com
www.discoveremg.com

Getting More from Your DJ

Dr. Don Galbo
The Music Revue DJ's,
Sound and Lighting Productions

Are you excited for your wedding day? Are you looking for a DJ company that will cater to all of your specific needs, work with you financially, and give you professional-grade sound, lighting, and customer service? Lucky for you, you're reading in the right place! My name is Dr. Don Galbo, also known as "Dr. Don" in the DJ industry. I am the owner of The Music Revue DJ's, Sound and Lighting Productions, LLC located in Newnan, Georgia, near Atlanta. Whether your reception is big or small, we will help you set up adequate equipment and give you an unforgettable experience. With our multiple systems, we cater our sound and lighting to what you need, and we will gladly make recommendations to what you really ought to have, tailoring the system and price to your true needs.

You will get more from us than you would with a regular DJ company. For example, a normal DJ company usually has one kind of setup, and you basically have to take it or leave it with no variation in system setup or price. Our intent is to cater as closely as possible to all of your entertainment needs. We do this by asking a lot of questions that elicit information to help us determine what your actual needs are. We don't want to bring a system that is too small or too big to your reception venue. As a company, we find ourselves in a unique position by having multiple systems. Because of this, we can transform to any event.

At The Music Revue DJ's, Sound and Lighting Productions, LLC, we want to make sure to cater to your financial needs as much as possible. There is no need for you to pay for things that you don't need. For instance, when you go to look for your wedding dress or tuxedo, the bridal shop doesn't make you buy one you cannot afford. They work with your budget to make something work for you, so you can still get something you will really enjoy wearing. That is the same approach my company takes. We want to know what your financial needs are, and then, we will adequately create a setup that includes sound and lighting, just for you.

None of this came overnight. There was a lot of time, planning, and learning that went into building this company. I have always loved music, and I first started DJing when I was 12 years old. I loved to listen to music and provided it for my friends when we went to the beach. I loved hearing it loud, especially with pristine, quality, pro audio equipment. Eventually, all of the pieces fell into place, and I went from one system to two, to three, to more, with exceptional sound and lighting equipment, as well. Additionally, I have always loved to see people have a good time.

With the DJ business, I go out there, and everybody is having a great time, glad to be at the event. People love what you do for them! Likewise, because we love what we do, we are very responsive and quick with getting back to our clients and getting requests up and ready for guests. We get the same treatment from our clients in return. We get immediate feedback about our services because our clients are so excited about the amazing time they just had. As we finish a job, we are already getting feedback online. This is a great feeling to have, especially when you have the personality and charisma to mix in with the music to make that happen. Making an event memorable and fun provides instant gratification, and it is a very rewarding profession. That is what motivates us to keep moving forward and providing exceptional entertainment services for our clients. Plus, DJing is also a stress-reliever from dentistry, and less stress is always nice!

Keeping motivated is easy when everything goes 100% right at a wedding. There was one reception that we recently did with about 500 guests in a very challenging venue. We had to unload farther away from the room than we would've liked, and we were upstairs on a balcony. We got all of the equipment in the room, set everything up, and once the music started playing, guests came up to us and said that they had never heard sound quality like what we had put out. Furthermore, we had an exceptional environment to do some really terrific things with lighting. We had a nice mixture of subtle but elegant LED lighting and some very exciting lights moving to the beat of the music. We introduced the bridal party to "Sirius" by The Alan Parson's Project (the Chicago Bulls introduction song), and we built up the excitement with the music and the lights. The guests went crazy. When the night was over, guests raved about our performance. The people that owned the venue, the crowd that was there, and the workers all said we were the best DJs they had ever seen. It was our first time working at this particular venue, and out of hundreds of DJs, we were the best. That's true success.

Even with all of the success, there have been some mishaps, as well. There have been plenty of times when something fails, and we have to instantly replace it and continue on. For this reason, we always make sure that we have backup equipment for everything on every truck and trailer that goes out. In Georgia, we tend to have a lot of power outages in the warmer months because of bad storms or tornados, so we have had a couple of occasions where we lost power and ended up bringing out a generator to keep the party going. Also, we have had speakers that have blown out in the middle of the night, and we have to replace them. Usually guests don't notice because we replace them so seamlessly.

Then, there are the occasions where the guests do notice a mistake. At one wedding, I had the bride and groom's first dance song all cued up and ready to go when, for some reason, the computer faulted. I ended up getting on the microphone and said that there had been a technical glitch. While I was trying to fix the problem, I told a couple of quick jokes and, within 30 to 40 seconds, the song was up and running. Despite this glitch, the rest of the wedding went great! As with all technology, it is common to have a mishap here and there, but we make sure to get it turned around as quickly and tactfully as possible.

Because of the possibility of mishaps, it is very important to find a professional DJ who has been in business for a long time. I am not trying to slam any of the newcomers, but unless they have taken some formal courses on how to maneuver and manipulate and control a wedding reception, it is just too easy to have a nightmare occur. I have heard too many horror stories about new DJs in the business that just don't have the concept of how to handle a wedding reception. They get into trouble and ruin a couple's perfect day. I recommend you find the best professionals you can have. It's your day, it's your dream, and you want to have professionals who are experienced. These DJs will make sure you get the type of result you want and deserve. Money shouldn't be an issue in this case. Don't cut corners and try to save; only hire the best.

Finding the perfect DJ doesn't happen in 10 or 15 minutes. It takes a little bit of time to do some research and find out who will mesh best with you and your fiancé. You want to get a feel for their personality, because if someone doesn't have any personality when you're having the first phone consultation, they are not going to have it on your wedding day. This brings up another point. Don't just rely on internet communication, and never hire anyone straight off of a website. You want to make sure that you talk to the individual involved with that company, get a feel for his or her personality, and then make your decision. Look for testimonials and try to get contact information of previous clients. This is a very powerful source to check because you will get a sense of what this individual or company is all about.

Nevertheless, hiring the best DJ doesn't just instantly make your reception successful and memorable. It is also very important to get your guests involved. My company offers a program called "DJ Intelligence," where the bride and groom can plan some details of their wedding and reception online. A great feature, which has resulted in exceptional feedback from brides, grooms, and guests, was opening up our music library to everyone attending the wedding. Brides and grooms love to have the ability to browse our music library and select songs they want to hear. We go one step further and incorporate the guests, as well. They have the same access to our music library as the bride and groom do, and we limit each guest to request one song through the online database. Guests are often excited when we play a song they requested, and they bring out their family and friends to dance to it. This interaction makes the night that much more entertaining and memorable.

At a wedding reception, there is such an eclectic crowd. People range from young children to teenagers to people in their sixties and seventies. So, when you are picking music for your reception, it is important that you not only pick songs that you like, but that you pick songs for your guests, as well. As a DJ, I want to please you, the bride and groom, first and foremost; however, it is a good idea to play music that everyone will like. This is another aspect that we can help you with, so don't worry!

Do not make the mistake of thinking that the DJ is only going to be providing the entertainment for the night and that the night is going to be successful just because of that. Ultimately, yes, this is how it will go. But things need to be planned and talked about in advance. The worst way you can sabotage your wedding reception is by not giving necessary information to your DJ, wedding planners, or any other vendors or individuals involved in reception planning. If you are very laid back and have not given your specifications to anyone, things can go in whatever direction, and the event becomes hard to control. If you're not going to be organized and plan ahead, you run the risk of having the reception get out of control—something that you probably won't want to happen.

Another thing that can put a damper on the celebratory mood of the reception is the toast. I always try to advise my bride and grooms to not let too many people get into the toast arena. It is just better if the best man and the maid or matron of honor give the toasts. If you open it up to too many people, it becomes hard to say no, and you wind up spending an hour with everybody making a toast. It really ruins the formality of the reception and cuts into the dance portion of the evening.

Finally, as I mentioned before, finding a professional DJ is something that should be taken seriously. The DJ business has evolved in good and bad ways. Professional DJs are more available than ever before; unfortunately, ever since the iPod revolution and the ability to download music, there have been a lot of new DJs that have just downloaded a lot of music, gone out and bought a few speakers, and tried to DJ, even though they do not have the personality for it. I find that a little frightening. If you want someone that is going to do more than just play music, you have to do your homework and investigate just how well these people present themselves. Hire people who not only know music, but when and how to play it. To me, it is a matter of finding someone with enough experience to do the job correctly, otherwise, why would you be hiring us in the first place?

The point of a professional DJ is to actually have someone who can handle your crowd, break the ice if necessary, tell a few jokes, put a few spins on things, and get people dancing. I really don't recommend that people try to run their own event with an iPod, unless all they want to have is shuffling music in the background. Beyond that, if you need any MC expertise, and you need someone who knows how to maneuver a particular event, whatever that event may be, a professional DJ is the way you need to go. If you really want to get the impact you are looking for, go pro!

So, if you do decide to hire a professional DJ service like The Music Revue DJ's, Sound and Lighting Productions, LLC, you are going to get a professional, quality entertainment service that will take care of all of your needs. It is our intention to provide the highest-quality service in entertainment for your wedding reception. It is also our desire to provide you with a service that you would like to have, and not what we would like for you. We feel that making your dream come true should be done in a joint manner, at a fair, reasonable price. So, let us take care of all your entertainment needs. From pristine sound to exceptional lighting to working with you financially, we will give you an unforgettable experience for you and your guests. We definitely look forward to meeting with you soon!

About Dr. Don

Dr. Don Galbo, better known as Dr. Don in DJ circles, has been in the DJ business for over thirty-five years. As a youngster in the late sixties, he was the one that always had the "portable turntable" with 45's in tow. If there was no music, he provided it. During College from 1972–1976, he was a campus radio station DJ and worked summers in some of the first "Disco" clubs in the New York City area. Back then, there were two turntables, a three channel mixer, and that was it.

While attending dental school at the University of Maryland School of Dentistry from 1978-1982, he was the campus DJ at the pub called The Synapse. Every Thursday night, he and about 400 battled students from all of the professional schools squeezed in for some much needed relaxation and dancing fun. Dr. Don provided the music and MCed all of the events scheduled. After developing a successful business in the Baltimore/Washington, D.C., area for three years, he moved to Southwest Georgia and began the business anew in the Columbus and Albany, Georgia, area.

After moving to the Atlanta, Georgia, area in 1985, he once again started the business anew and branded it with the name "The Music Revue DJ's, Sound and Lighting Productions, LLC. I guess one might say that a DJ that has stayed in the business that long, and succeeded in three different markets, must be pretty good. As the technologies have changed in the business, he has moved along with it. His company was one of the first in the US to embrace computerization and the mp3 format. Now, all of the company music is on hard drives. In addition, he has stayed current on all of the latest DMX lighting, and the LED revolution.

Dr. Don Galbo
The Music Revue DJ's, Sound and Lighting Productions
drdonthedj@gmail.com
www.themusicrevuedjs.com

A Moral Obligation

Steve "Champagne" Sala
A Shining Star Production

Do you want a dedicated, hard-working DJ who has been in the business for a long time and is looking out for what you want on your wedding day? You have come to the right place! My name is Steve "Champagne" Sala, and I am the owner of A Shining Star Production, located in Ocala, Florida. For me, DJing is all about passion. It is something that I work to improve upon on a daily basis. I am committed to listening to my clients and giving them time-tested advice to make their receptions what they have always dreamed of. When I work with you, your event is my singular, primary focus. What's unique about A Shining Star Productions is that we make sure to focus on one event at a time, in order to get every "I" dotted, "T" crossed, and bride and groom left smiling!

My passion for music and entertainment started at the age of six, when I watched the labels spin around on records while pretending to be Casey Kasem. One of my closest friends and I even had our own little radio show, where we played all the latest hits. My first promotion came when I started DJing in a local skating rink at the age of 12! I enjoyed performing at skating rinks and apparently did a decent job, because next thing you know, I was live on the radio, and then spinning at hot night clubs in Atlanta. One thing just led to the next, but what I loved the most about all these experiences was the effect I was able to have on people's lives. Even as a drummer in a band on tour, when I watched the pros interact and influence the audience, I was intrigued and knew that this was the right business for me. All of those experiences and observations allowed me to develop my company in a way that is, first and foremost, client focused.

Now, as the owner of a professional DJ company, I want to work with you by combining your vision and my experience to make your party as memorable and unforgettable as possible. I want to personally make sure that your wedding is completely unique to you, and that you are happy with the whole night from beginning to end. I do weddings for the simple reason that it puts smiles on people's faces and lasting memories in their hearts. A wedding is supposed to be the most special day of your life. The memories created (whether good or bad) during this time are going to last forever. I take the responsibility of making sure that you remember your wedding in a positive way. If I can make you and your families and friends smile for four or five hours, I will be pleased. The challenge of pulling off the biggest night of your life gives me a rush, and I love it. I'm very passionate about what I do, and I aim to see everything turn out the best way it possibly could. I love making people dance, and I love being a part of their celebration.

Making people happy isn't always easy, but it is definitely attainable. I once worked with a couple where the groom was Jewish. Despite being Jewish, the groom did not want a Jewish wedding. As you can imagine, his entire family was pushing him to honor all the Jewish customs during the reception, but he really did not want to. At the reception, there was a disagreement. Being a DJ who's attuned to my clients, I could just see the tension brewing. The parents were adamant about having things done their way, and the groom was just as strong willed about having things done the way he wanted them. The family of the groom wrongly assumed that he would eventually oblige and do things the way they wanted. This was not the case. Neither the groom nor his wife felt the need to compromise.

So, when I saw the tensions about to come to a head, I changed the mood through timing, song selection, and entertainment, and completely had the family forgetting about their religious differences. This story shows how a great DJ can anticipate problems and fix them quickly and seamlessly. I could sense that the reception was turning into a possible fistfight, and was able to avoid that by being a great MC and setting up re-directing music at the appropriate time.

A lot of DJs ere in thinking that if they just play the latest chart-topping songs, everybody will get up and dance. Unfortunately, that doesn't always work. It's more about *when* to play certain songs, rather than what songs to play. If a crowd isn't motivated, a DJ should know how to motivate them without being up in their face. A good DJ should have activities up their sleeves that everyone can participate in. When looking for a legitimate DJ, look for one that constantly observes crowds and reads their energy. Based upon his observations, a good DJ makes the best decisions to keep as many people on the dance floor as possible.

I give complete and total effort when doing a reception. Some people may think that just because they purchase a cheaper wedding package from me, I don't try as hard to make their night successful. This is not true by any means! Trust me, it is physically impossible for me give less than 100% of my effort for each package. Not only is this because I have a strong passion and sense of moral obligation to make sure what should be the best day of your life *is* the best day of your life, but also because the success of my business depends on the success of your event. What good would it do me to not give 100%? I strive to work around people's budgets, but please don't assume that the cheaper the package, the worse service you get, and the more expensive the package, the better service you get. I can't say the same for other DJs, however. Rest assured, with A Shining Star Production, I personally guarantee you that I will take care of your night and make it as special as possible—no matter who you are or what you pay.

A deep sense of pride and moral obligation to one's clients is something you cannot get with a wannabe DJ. You need to be aware of these people because there are a lot of them out there giving professional DJs a bad name! These DJ wannabes download a bunch of music for free off the internet, stick it in their laptop, and profess to be "a professional DJ." In reality, they don't have a clue about reading a room, timing, MCing, making announcements properly, and coordinating with the photographer and videographer about the best locations for pictures, grand entrances, and dance floor activities. Just because you may have seen a guy in a club or in some small venue playing music, it doesn't mean he is qualified to handle your wedding. Leave the most memorable night of your life to the professionals. You don't want to learn this lesson the hard way.

Make sure you hire the right DJ. Sometimes, brides and grooms don't understand what a DJ does or how they do it—knowing music, having crowd-reading experience, and maintaining equipment. Because they are uneducated, when a price seems higher than what they expected, they think it is a rip off. When considering cost, please keep in mind that wedding receptions last between four and six hours. Also, DJs have behind-the-scenes preparations they do to ensure your event runs smoothly and that there are no surprises. Although you may not see it, a good DJ is spending countless hours making sure that your reception is special. However, a good DJ also makes his job look easy, and will not stress you out by explaining all of the hard work he is doing to make your night go off without a hitch. So, don't rely on price alone. Keep in mind the adage "you get what you pay for." I know it's an old saying, but it is definitely true.

Another tip I can give you is to work with your DJ on the planning process. You don't have to call the DJ every other day or every week, just spend time with the DJ like you would any other vendor. Don't be afraid to sit down with your DJ and take the time to lay out your actual reception. Make sure that you always coordinate with your DJ and other personnel involved in the wedding. A sign of a bad DJ is one that is not open to working with you. A good DJ should be eager to hear all of your ideas and active in asking you questions to get a clearer idea of your vision for the night. The worst thing you can do is not coordinate with everyone in advance. If you don't do your homework, you will have a great deal of stress on your wedding day, and everyone will be running around like chickens with their heads cut off, frantically trying to make your day special. The most successful receptions I've done are ones in which the bride and the groom sat down with me in advance to make sure their vision was clearly communicated and a plan of execution was established.

Planning also helps your photographer and videographer. For them to capture those special moments, the DJ is the one with the ability to stage those moments. If the DJ is doing something fun that makes everybody laugh, or everybody dance, the photographer has great pictures besides the still shots outside the church. A good DJ will coordinate these events so that the photographer is ready to go and not scrambling to capture these special times. Sure, the photographer takes the shots, but it's the DJ's ability to create a fun and comfortable atmosphere that creates the smiles for the shots.

Atmosphere is also very important. Lighting, up lighting, and other small details make a huge difference in a venue's ambience. I'm not talking about tacky Radio Shack lighting or something really cheap you can rent. I'm talking about high-quality, classy lighting that creates a definite mood. Think about it: There's a reason why night clubs don't have bright lights that illuminate everyone dancing. They want close, intimate encounters to occur, so the lighting is often dark and punctuated by bold, flashing colors. So, if you're having an I-want-the-dance- party-of-my-life kind of reception, then lighting and atmosphere are definitely big factors affecting the success of your event. If you make the room and the dance floor look enticing, then, of course, without having to give it any thought, people will naturally get in the mood.

When it is all said and done, you can make your wedding day as special and unique as you want. There are so many options to cater to you and your guests. It is up to you how you want to do things, but ultimately up to your vendors to make it happen. So, don't learn the hard way, hire legitimate, professional service providers. A good DJ will guide you through the planning process and, as a result of their experience in the industry, offer you suggestions along the way. With my unshakable work ethic and passion for making your reception a success, you can be sure that you will have a relaxing and incredibly fun time with A Shining Star Production in the DJ booth! For more information about our services, please feel free to look us up on the web at www.ashiningstarproduction.com. In the meantime, I can't wait to help you plan your wedding and entertain you and your guests all night long!

About Steve Sala

Started out in 1976 at the age of 12, DJjing at skating rinks.
1977: Won first award from Georgia Music Education Association (Won 11 awards in all 1977–1981)
1980–1983: USAF Tactical Air Command Base talent show winner three years straight.
1984–1988: Tour drummer with national recording acts.
1989: Founded A Shining Star Production
1989–Present: Owner and president of A Shining Star Production.
1990–Present: As owner and programmer, have performed with or was sound/lighting technician for the following bands: Joan Jett, Keith Sweat, New Edition, Quiet Riot, Romantics, Fuel, Drowning Pool, Adler's Appetite (Steven Adler from Guns N Roses and his All-Star Band), and Alien Ant Farm, just to name a few.
1996 Rothmeyer School of Lighting Design
Steve Sala

A Shining Star Production

352-804-4056

www.ashiningstarproduction.com

Raising the Bar for Your Day

Barry Reynolds
DJ Wizard Entertainment

A professional DJ service's main goal is to give you the successful event of your dreams by providing good quality entertainment. You want to look for a DJ who works with you to help plan the perfect entertainment for your special day. My name is Barry Reynolds, and I am the proud owner of DJ Wizard Entertainment, located in Bryan, Ohio. We are the kind of company you are looking for.

At DJ Wizard Entertainment, our goal is to raise the bar to the ultimate standard in the entertainment industry by providing you with the highest level of professional, personalized service available. We do this by using the latest technology and services to provide an exciting and memorable experience for you and your guests.

Unlike other DJs who just copy one another, we've developed a service where all of our packages can be customized to your needs so that your day is truly unique. Even our lighting options are unlike any others out there. Each package we offer is different, as it is tailored to your reception. We subscribe to the same music that the radio stations get, so all of our music is current and radio edited, which means it is family friendly. Furthermore, we use air cards or wireless networks (when available), so we can always download music requests on the spot if we don't have it.

None of the other DJ services in this area offer anything like that.

We religiously get to our shows early in case of unforeseen difficulties. We like to have time to set up, make sure all the lights are focused and working correctly, and, most importantly, to make sure we don't have any surprises with the sound system. We typically are set up and ready to go at least an hour before your reception even starts. Because of our meticulous planning process, when the event begins, we already have our format laid out. This is just one more thing a professional will do for your event to make the evening flow properly.

The format, which we create with you, includes what's going to happen from the time when you and your bridal party come through the door and how the evening is expected to go to the end when everybody is leaving to go home. Typically, the bride and groom have a grand entrance, which leads right into the usual ceremonies, such as the first dance, cake cutting, father/daughter dance, bouquet toss, and much more. Throughout the evening, we read your crowd to play the appropriate music to keep them on the dance floor.

Sometimes, things don't always go as planned—especially when technology is involved. One incident I will never forget is when I had an outside gig booked in the early days of our career.

Since we were a young company, we didn't have the luxury of experience or the cash flow to buy top-quality equipment to help us avoid common mistakes. (Just another thing your DJ should have is quality tools to work with.) Things started out fine. We were blasting out tunes and everybody was having a great time. All of the sudden, a DJ's worst nightmare occurred—dead silence! I feared that I had lost an amp.

Fortunately, we were only about 10 miles from my house, so I managed to drive back and get our other system. We got it loaded in the trailer and went to start the vehicle, but of course, it wouldn't start. It took us over an hour to get the car started. Once we finally got back to the event with the new system, we discovered it was actually the speakers that were blown. So, we headed back home to get our other speakers.

This time, we took my friend's vehicle back to the event. It was a little Geo Tracker, so you can imagine the difficulties we faced trying to put 15-inch Yamaha monitor speakers in the back with three of us in the car. More troubles occurred when the water pump on the Geo started leaking, and it started overheating. We were able to limp it back. Once we got back to the event, we managed to set up quickly and get the party going again. To make up for the inconvenience, we gladly played an extra two hours. Everyone ended up having a great time, but it was definitely the worst thing that ever happened to us. Since this experience, we've been diligent about getting to shows early and testing our equipment. We also make sure that we have backup equipment on hand, just in case!

Fortunately, things like that don't happen very often. If something like that was to occur, though, it is the DJ's responsibility to get the problems fixed immediately. You will want to hire a DJ you can trust, and then everything should be fine. A professional DJ orchestrates your entire night for you, and makes the event run smoothly. Make sure that you go over playlists with your DJ in advance. It is important to make it known what songs you would like played or not played at your reception. However, don't limit the DJ too much. After all, we are professionals, and professionals know how to handle a crowd and keep them on the dance floor all night long. Try to remember; although this is your event, you do have guests to consider. I would be willing to guess they don't all like the same music you do. There is the possibility that they would like to hear something they like, too.

Finding a DJ who will keep your dance floor full can sometimes be a difficult task. After all, there are many DJs out there who are complacent and offer much of the same thing. How do you know which one to pick? Well, don't pick one that is the same as everyone else. Ask for references. Go with someone who will put a unique spin on your reception to make it fun, someone whose hands you feel comfortable leaving your event in. Let's face it—if your guests are bored, your event will be boring, and, although it will be remembered, I'll bet it won't be remembered the way you had hoped it would be.

Here's something different we have done in the past that is fun and memorable—a hog trough dance. If a younger sibling gets married before an older one, the older sibling has to do a dance inside a hog trough to some sort of funny song (that was picked out by the younger sibling) during the actual reception. It is a fun way to tease the older sibling for not being married yet. Guests always have a good time with this tradition, but we also have many more ideas to share with our clients that will make their wedding stand out and be remembered. Your DJ should be creative and be able to make some fun suggestions for you to add to your event.

At DJ Wizard, we pride ourselves in making your special event all it should be and more. From the time you hire us, to the time we perform your event, we are available to work with you. We will also help with suggestions and scheduling the festivities for your party. We will do whatever it takes to make your event a success. You will feel comfortable knowing that we encourage you to call us at any time to answer questions and guide you along the way.

Don't pick a DJ just because he or she is cheap. Price is important, but even more important is what you actually get for the hard-earned dollar you are investing. This is a get-what-you-pay-for business. Do you want someone who will just show up to play music and pray that no technical difficulties occur? Or, would you rather have a DJ who is professional, experienced, works with you on planning, and keeps your dance floor packed from start to finish? DJ Wizard knows that unforgettable events take good planning, and that is what we will do for all our clients.

Although the DJ has the ultimate responsibility of making your event fun and memorable, there are some actions that you can take to ensure that your wedding reception is successful. It is always good to interact with your guests. Believe it or not, your presence plays an integral part in keeping things going and getting people on the dance floor! So be present with a positive attitude. Don't forget to let loose and have fun!

Another thing to take into consideration is getting through the classic traditions at a decent pace, so that everybody can enjoy the rest of the evening. Classic traditions such as toasts, media presentations, cake cutting, first dances, and table visits are all important wedding protocol, but manage your time wisely. The faster that the protocol can get accomplished, the faster your guests can get on the dance floor and start celebrating with you.

All in all, it is important to hire the right entertainment for your event. DJ Wizard was established as (and still is) a personalized, professional, full-service entertainment company that takes pride in the personalization of each of our client's receptions. Every couple is different, so it is important that every reception reflects what makes them unique. We are on the cutting edge of innovation with our brilliant light shows that illuminate the dance floor with vivid beams and patterns of light that dance, flash, and chase to the rhythmic, pulsating beat of our crystal-clear, mega-power audio systems. We pride ourselves on definitely having what it takes to give our clients and their guests an awesome, complete sound and light experience. We are sure you will be more than just excited at what we have to offer! DJ Wizard is the kind of company that will work with you from start to finish. We are innovative and do what it takes to keep the experience we offer fresh and exciting.

I believe you will find this is the kind of service you are looking for to make your big day successful.

Best wishes, and I hope this has helped you grasp some better insight into the selection of the right DJ service for your event.

Remember, you only get to get it right once.

About Barry Reynolds

I started my company, DJ Wizard Entertainment, with my wife Mary because I love music and because we were tired of all the same old things out there. We wanted to create a personalized service that was a cut above what everyone else was offer-  ing. We hand pick all our equipment to make sure we can provide an experience that is second to none.

We have been doing this for six years now, and we have never had any disappointed clients. Our sound and light shows get compliments wherever we do a show.

Look for us on the web, send us an e-mail, or give us a call. We would love to show you what we can do for your big day.

Barry Reynolds
DJ Wizard Entertainment
419–630–8931
info@mobiledjwizard.com
www.mobiledjwizard.com

The Ingredients for Awesome Entertainment at Your Wedding

Chad Day
Have A Nice Day Mobile Entertainment

*Y*our wedding day is coming up, and you need to be the center of attention. Let me put the spotlight on you and your fiancé so your dreams can come true and your reception will be remembered forever. My name is Chad Day, and I am the owner of Have A Nice Day Mobile Entertainment in Owensboro, Kentucky. I am a professionally trained master of ceremonies and have been in the DJ scene since 2001. Back then, I began shadowing other DJs for wedding receptions; and from that, I quickly learned what it takes to make every wedding reception unique, how to engage an audience, and how to pay attention to even the smallest details to ensure a successful reception.

As time went on, I was able to purchase my own sound and lighting equipment and began subcontracting for different DJ companies in Kentucky and the Cincinnati, Ohio, area. Finally, in 2011, my dream job as a self-employed entrepreneur at Have A Nice Day Mobile Entertainment became a reality. Since then, I have been putting newlyweds in the spotlight, making their special night the most memorable celebration of their life, and I am very passionate about doing that! I strive to provide my clients and their guests with a quality and unforgettable experience. You will quickly learn that all of the entertainment for your reception is completely under control, and you can spend your time on other things in the wedding- and reception-planning process.

Let me take the stress away from planning entertainment for your reception. I make sure to cater my services to your specific needs. I want to make your wedding completely unique to you. After all, it is your wedding—you should have things in your reception that reflect the kind of couple you are. I want to make sure that I ask you what is important to you. I am very upfront and am willing to transform my style to yours. For example, if you want a lot of guest participation, because that is the kind of person you are, I can make that happen.

There was one instance in which I could not meet with the future bride and groom because of their geographic restrictions. I asked them what kind of reception they wanted, and they wished to have a ton of guest participation while they were taking pictures after the ceremony. So, while everyone was enjoying the cocktail hour, I asked who was with the bride and who was with the groom. Ultimately, I wanted to bring both sides of their families together.

Why, you may ask? Because your wedding is a celebration of you and your brand-new spouse joining each other in your journey to a lifetime of happiness TOGETHER. This made everyone feel as if they were part of the same family! After some more crowd interaction, I asked who had traveled the furthest. This had many people telling others who they were and where they were from.

By the end of the night, there were people who were introducing themselves to folks that they didn't even know. The guests and the bride and groom wound up very happy, and I was even told that the reception wouldn't have been a success without me. However, if you do not want to have a heavy-participation reception, that is just fine. By using my easy-to-use online planning tools on my website, you can literally choose anything and everything for your night. But don't worry; I can help you along the way, as well! It doesn't have to be all up to you if you don't want it that way!

Remember, Have A Nice Day Mobile Entertainment pays particular attention to all of your special needs; this is the main ingredient to look for when searching for a DJ. You need a DJ who has the ability to plan with the photographer, videographer, and other vendors. When all of your vendors are in tune with each other, your celebration runs like a well-oiled machine! You need to have someone whom you can trust with all of your entertainment wants and needs, and someone who will listen to you and make your wedding one for the ages.

For example, there was one time when a couple did not choose to go with my services for their wedding. Some time into the reception with the other DJ, however, there was an equipment failure, and the couple ended up calling me to get my backup equipment over to the reception. At the end of the night, they paid me for saving their reception and regretted not choosing me from the beginning. Two things came from this experience that I can share with you. First of all, make sure you budget enough for your entertainment. Cheaper is not better by any means! You get what you pay for, so don't skimp out on your DJ. Spend the extra money to make your night that much more unforgettable. Second of all, paying attention to details is a must. Equipment failure is something that I am prepared for, considering that I have a backup for everything. The fact that I was able to bring over my equipment to keep the reception going was huge in that couple's eyes. I took time out of my evening to go and fix the situation, which should have initially required close attention and planning for the worst. That is what I do. I take minor things that you might not think of, and make sure that there are easy solutions to keep you and your guests happy and on the dance floor.

There was another instance in which the bride and groom didn't let the person who was supposed to bless the meal know that he was elected for the job. There were obviously a thousand different things going through their minds throughout planning their reception, and they forgot to ask him if he would say the blessing. I had the person's name for the duty in my notes, so I knew whom I was supposed to locate. I spent 15 minutes trying to hunt him down, even making announcements and asking other guests if they had seen him. I wanted to make sure he was prepared for when he would be blessing the meal. Well, it turns out he was nowhere to be found! The entire bridal party arrived in their limousine, and as I was lining them all up and giving instructions for their grand entrance, I asked if they had seen him. I informed the bride and groom of the situation. Their eyes grew as big as quarters, and their jaws almost hit the floor!

Immediately after the introduction and a quick photo session of the bridal party behind the bridal table, there was to be a blessing and the Captain's Call dinner was to begin. I could tell that they were close to panic, and everyone was hungry. They couldn't think of anyone else that would want to get on the microphone and give the blessing. They didn't need the stress and just wanted to have dinner, their formalities, and get on with the party! This is where I volunteered to bless the meal. I immediately sensed a relief, and they said that they would greatly appreciate it if I would go ahead and do it. I remember saying, "Absolutely, no problem," and I'll admit it, seeing their relaxed expression with smiles on their faces made me feel great. Everything went off without a hitch, and their celebration was a great success. We later learned that the person who was originally supposed to bless the meal had to run to his hotel to pick up their gift during cocktail hour, and after he arrived, it wound up being a big laugh!

What you can learn from this story is to make sure that you find an MC who is capable of solving problems and thinking on the fly. There is only one way to get to that level, and it is through training and experience. The DJ that wants to sell their service to you by telling you that they have 30,000 songs and advertising that they are "the best" isn't always going to be able to get you through a sticky situation like this! Anyone can buy the equipment and the music, but it takes talent and experience to turn challenges into success.

Another challenge that requires skill is the ability to keep your guests dancing all night long, especially when your guests will have a wide variety of music tastes. Take it from me, and make sure you consider your other guests when picking out music! For instance, if you are a rocker through and through, and that is all you like, that could very well be all you will want. You will probably believe that rock music is what everyone else wants to hear, too. That is a common mistake that many couples make. It is best to include some of the older people (especially if you are a younger couple) because older people can get some enjoyment out of hearing a couple of older songs during the cocktail hour or dinner. This makes everyone happy. If everybody can hear a little snippet of their type of music, that makes for a great time for all.

Again, this may sound like a difficult task, but luckily for you, my website provides all of the tools necessary to pick songs for your reception. You are able to see what the top music requests are for a wedding, what songs are suggested for a specific dance (i.e., mother/son or father/daughter), and you can pick from an extensive library of music. This is a great thing because you may come across songs that you would not have otherwise thought of if they were not right in front of you.

However, music does not make the entire reception. It is definitely a big part of your night, but there are other things that can make your wedding day a lot easier on you and your guests. One thing that I have seen, something I did at my own wedding, was to get the pictures with your soon-to-be spouse out of the way before the actual ceremony. Yes, there are couples out there who prefer the traditional way and will not see each other before the ceremony. This is not a bad thing at all. But by having pictures taken before the ceremony, you will have more time to enjoy the celebration after the wedding. Pictures won't take as long with your parents, grandparents, and other relatives because you took some with your spouse and bridal party earlier on. It is as easy as saying to your photographer, "We still want to have our special moment, but the special moment is just going to be sooner than the ceremony."

Also, it is really nice for your guests to have drinks and hors d'oeuvres before the bridal party arrives at the reception hall. You have probably been in that situation where you go to a reception and you are standing around with a bunch of other people with nothing to do. Choose to get your guests involved a little bit. Whether that is by having food and drinks served during that time or having your DJ interact with the guests, make it worthwhile for your guests. That is the most important thing.

All in all, it is definitely worth checking out Have A Nice Day Mobile Entertainment. From beginning to end, I will be in charge of your entertainment and will take care of you, so you don't have to stress. When you meet with me, you know that you are getting me as your DJ. I don't have eight other DJs that I send out, so you will actually meet with me, your DJ. I don't necessarily want to say quantity over quality—but sometimes that is exactly what happens. This is a single operation that I am running, but I make sure that I am very in tune with all of your needs and wants so that you can get the most memorable reception ever. With my talent and passion for making your night special, specifically for you, you and your guests will have an incredible night. I look forward to talking with you soon.

About Chad Day

I am a DJ and Master of Ceremonies professionally trained by the one-and-only Mike Manzi of the Greater Cincinnati area. I got my start in 2001 while I was a college student looking to earn a few extra bucks on the weekends. I began by shadowing other great

DJ entertainers' performances, mainly for wedding receptions. I quickly learned what it takes to make every wedding reception unique, how to engage an audience, and how to pay attention to every small detail to ensure a very successful and fun celebration. I earned my way into being ready to take on gigs on my own. As I honed my skills as a professional entertainer, I realized that I am fortunate to have the unique talent that it takes to be great in this field. Eventually, I was able to purchase my own sound and lighting equipment and began sub-contracting for a few different DJ companies.

I graduated from Northern Kentucky University in 2005 with a Bachelor of Science in Marketing and moved from Northern Kentucky to Owensboro, Kentucky, in 2006. I pursued my dream of self-employment and formed Have A Nice Day Mobile Entertainment in 2011. Focusing on the bride and groom, making them the center of attention and fulfilling their desires, has been the recipe for many happy newlyweds, and also for their family and closest friends. I have a true passion for helping my clients realize their ultimate dreams, and it is my goal to be the main reason that their event is one that will be remembered forever. To ensure the wedding reception of your dreams, please visit us on the web or give us a call. You and your guests will be impressed...guaranteed!

Have A Nice Day Mobile Entertainment
270–316–8077
cday@haveanicedayme.com
www.haveanicedayme.com

Shhh! There's No Secret to Being a DJ

Mike Gintella
Mike's Light and Sound

My name is Mike Gintella, and I am the owner of Mike's Light and Sound, along with BridesDJ.com and DJreferral.com, all based out of Shreveport, Louisiana. Although there is no secret to DJing, it's shocking how few DJs get it right. DJing is not just about music; it's about taking care of clients and handling situations with confidence and grace. During the initial meeting I have with my clients, I get to know them, understand their interests, likes and dislikes, and how they envision their wedding reception. From there, I creatively construct a plan that fits their needs. This is a big feature of my company, and something that we continue to practice day in and day out. We hold our clients in such high regard because I personally feel that a wedding day is specifically for you, the bride and groom, and no one else. With us, you get exactly what you want for your reception; no one else can say otherwise.

My road to becoming a DJ started when I was about 13 years old. I started singing on the street corners of New Jersey for fun. Soon after, I began playing the guitar and learning how to back up my vocals with instruments. During this time, I developed my voice to a point where people would actually pay to hear me. After being a front man for many working bands, I joined the Air Force and, once again, was the front man for several bands while working in nightclubs. I met my wife, who has a beautiful singing voice, and once I left the Air Force, we traveled the country singing and playing music. With my wife's natural gift to sing and play the piano, and my talent at guitar and being a front man, we had a unique blend of music and comedy. I knew we had something special when people would drive a couple hundred miles just to see us. We got so big that we even shared the stage with big names like Tony Bennett and Ronnie Milsap. It was definitely a neat experience.

Once we moved to Shreveport, we started doing live entertainment for weddings, parties, private clubs, and corporate events. We quickly became popular, and in 1985, we decided to open a music store. We actually ended up with two music stores at one point, selling sound systems, guitars, drums, keyboards, and other musical things. In addition to selling musical gear, we sold ourselves by performing at weddings. This happened because soon after the store's opening, in 1986, we were getting calls asking for DJs. Although I had no equipment of my own, I couldn't say no, so I started booking DJs who were our clients at weddings. Fate was on my side. I was able to buy back a complete DJ set from a customer who bought it but quit three months later. After this, we had the passion, and now the equipment, so we started our formal operation. Mike's Light and Sound very quickly became the most popular DJs in the area. The wedding niche really took off, and I started making it a point to go to as many DJ seminars across the country as possible in order to hone my skills. To this day, I still attend seminars to improve my craft and service to my clients. Sadly, I don't always see a lot of other DJs, most of the time there are no other DJs from the Shreveport area at these seminars. I don't understand this, and think it is a huge mistake on their part because, as DJs, we all need to keep learning how to be better performers. If a DJ doesn't care to improve himself, it is likely he or she will not care to improve your wedding.

I believe seminars are key to understanding how to run a successful wedding reception. By implementing what we learn at seminars, and by observing and learning what's happening on the national scene, we are able to craft some unique wedding traditions for you and your fiancé's interests. "Protocols" are the typical activities that you see at a wedding reception—first dance, dance with parents, cake cutting, blessings, toasts, etcetera. The structure and timing of protocols can either thrill your guests or kill them with boredom. Weddings are expensive, and for that reason, I feel that it's our job at Mike's Light and Sound to move the protocols along at a good clip in order to keep guests interested and wondering what is going to happen next.

When I talk with my clients, I explain to them the difference between a legitimate, professional DJ, and a 12-year-old kid with an iPod and sound system. The main question is, "Will the inexperienced iPod DJ keep the night organized and fun, or will it be a disaster in which all the guests leave early out of boredom?" Because of my many years of experience, I can confidently tell you that the iPod DJ will not be able to keep your event entertaining. Your special day will just be one predictably boring incident after another. There will be no light commentary, announcements, or personality to break the monotony. By hiring a professional DJ, you get the comfort of knowing everything will be taken care of by someone whose livelihood depends on the success of your event. A professional DJ knows what they are doing and will do anything to ensure you and your spouse are elated at the end of the night.

Another important detail we keep a close eye on is making sure we know the whereabouts of your parents and other important people involved in the wedding. Making sure these people don't "disappear" and miss their opportunity to dance with you, or do other scheduled activities at the reception, is something that sets us apart from run-of-the-mill DJs. We don't want you stressed out, taking time from the fun to search for people. That is our job: to absorb your stress so you can enjoy yourself. With the precision of a search-and-rescue team, we always make sure that key people are around for the appropriate portion of the evening. This may seem like a small detail, but it is a critical variable to keep the reception moving smoothly and create a stress-free environment for you and your mate.

The single best piece of advice I can give you to make your reception wildly successful and unforgettable is for both of you (bride and groom) to be on the dance floor dancing away. The more that you are on the dance floor, the more guests will come and dance with you. When the dance floor is packed with people radiating off the newlyweds' glow, the entire reception is fun, and everyone has a great time. When the bride and groom are hanging out at the bar talking with people, or outside smoking for the majority of the night, the dance floor is empty. A bride and groom not interested in letting loose and having fun on the dance floor can easily kill the reception because guests look to them to be their leaders for the night. We encourage our brides and grooms and their wedding parties to be a part of the celebration, not just paying for it! When guests see you and your bridal party on the dance floor having fun, dancing, and leading activities, the fun is contagious and creates many unforgettable lifelong memories.

On the other hand, while it is great to have fun, don't have too much fun. In other words, don't get drunk! If the bride, groom, or other major wedding player at the reception is drunk, terrible things can happen. I have seen broken bones, heart attacks, and much more at receptions because key people are really drunk. These debacles bring the festivities to an instant end, and make your guests feel very uncomfortable. Have fun but stay coherent! You do not have to abstain from drinking, but make sure you are not out of control. Also, make sure you eat at your own wedding. This may sound like a no brainer, but I have seen some dinner set-ups at receptions where the guests eat before the bride and groom even arrive. This arrangement is problematic because the bride and groom end up not eating since everyone wants to talk to them when they arrive. Without eating, you will not have the energy to enjoy the night, and if you decide to drink alcohol, your tolerance will be much lower. Please, do not get stuck in bad situations that are easily preventable. Make sure you eat and don't drink too much alcohol.

At Mike's Light and Sound, we definitely make sure to bring up potential problems with our clients. There are plenty of wedding disasters on YouTube, and we watch these videos not to laugh, but to learn what not to do! Also, by watching these videos, we learn how to prevent disasters. After doing over a thousand weddings, we have plenty of experience with what makes a reception rock, but we just want to make sure couples are aware that there is a possibility that catastrophes may happen, despite the best planning. When we sit down, I will give your our game plan on how to avoid potentially devastating situations. By pedantically working with our clients before the big day, we develop a mutually agreed upon plan to put in place before the festivities begin.

But, again, it's all about having fun, enjoying yourself, and having your guests enjoy themselves as well. One fun way to do this is with customs! Over the years, we have seen some very cool customs at wedding receptions that bring a lot of fun to the party. Though we are based six hours away from New Orleans, the simple fact that we are in Louisiana makes Mardi Gras customs acceptable. For example, there is a line dance that people love to do around here, and that I do at many weddings. Here's how it goes. Before the reception, the bride and groom get a couple of umbrellas and fix them up nice and fancy. Then, at the reception, they are in the front of the line while the guests line up behind them, kind of like a train line, and the line snakes around the building while the umbrellas are twirling and Cajun music is playing. While they are circling the building, guests take their napkins and twirl them over their heads and dance. This is just one of the many simple and fun activities we can help you with to make your wedding fun and memorable.

Additionally, I have seen people come to weddings in Mardi Gras costumes, which is fun for everyone. It definitely adds a unique feel to the reception and makes for great photos. One thing that I suggest to brides and grooms that some have never heard of, but later found fun, is the dollar dance. At the very beginning of the dancing portion of the evening, I make an announcement saying that this is the only time the guests will have to dance with the bride and groom. However, they will have to pay for it! In a good-humored manner, people bring up money, whether it is a one-dollar bill, five dollars, or a hundred, put it in a basket and dance with the bride or groom. This is a great idea to get your guests involved and allow them a fun opportunity for photos with the bride and groom. If this isn't something that appeals to you, that's okay; we have many more unique ideas that are fun and romantic!

For instance, many of my clients request the Generation Dance. I invite all of the married couples onto the dance floor and begin to play a timeless love song. Periodically through the song, couples are eliminated from the dance floor based on how long they have been married. The longer the couple has been together, the longer they stay out on the dance floor. This goes on until there is just one couple left dancing. I ask the remaining couple to give a little history about their marriage and to give the newlyweds some advice. Depending on the couple standing, is the story can be funny, religious, or dirty, but everyone has a great time with it. Again, if you think that some of the dances I described are not for you, remember, I have many more to share with you. However, the primary goal of these dances is to get people involved. The dances are fun, memorable, and make for some great photo opportunities that you will appreciate for years to come. Don't forget—FUN is contagious!

In the end, however, it is important that you select activities that you want to have at your wedding reception. It's your special day, and no one can tell you otherwise. Don't take the stress on all by yourself, however. Hire a fantastic, professional DJ so that you can enjoy the fun, instead of being stressed out, wondering if things will turn out okay. Because of our extensive experience and professionalism, we at Mike's Light and Sound can ensure a truly unforgettable, entertaining reception experience that will uniquely cater to your needs, wants, and interests. I look forward to meeting with you soon to help you plan the next steps of your special day!

You can contact me at BridesDJ@gmail.com or MikesLights@aol.com, or just call us at 318–861–3669.

May your upcoming wedding be blessed and a blast!

About Mike Gintella

After meeting many professionals, such as doctors, CEOs, and attorneys, who have listened to me sing and play my guitar for many years and who told me they wished they had my talent, I feel pretty good about myself.

Before I started my DJ business, I worked in private clubs, restaurants, and hotels, mostly as a duet with my wife Joan. It was great because we were always in demand and made a good living playing music and entertaining folks from all walks of life and levels of success. Other musicians in the area could never understand how we could live such a comfortable life with a new house, new cars, furniture, etc. What they never figured out is it is not just about playing music, it's about how to keep people interested in what you are doing—whether it is because of the music itself or our ability to keep people laughing at our antics, many of our clients have become life-long friends.

In 1979, we were approached by Johnny Carson's producer, Stan Irwin, who had been hired to bring in acts for the Star Theatre at the LeBossier Hotel in Bossier City, La.

He felt that we were perfect to be able to follow the styles of all the name entertainers he was bringing in, such as Tony Bennett, Marty Robbins, Lou Rawls, Ronnie Milsap, and The Mills Brothers. All were top-notch, in-demand entertainers. Of course, I jumped at the opportunity. Stan made sure we got to meet and eat breakfast and converse with them all for about a year.

One night we visited with Paul Stanley from Kiss for about an hour, hung out with The Marshall Tucker band for three day, lunched with professional wrestlers, and had a famous actor thrown out of one establishment (won't mention names). George Carlin was a trip; James Burton (Elvis Presley's guitar player) is still a friend; Jimmy Dean (sausage king and singer) was a regular. Jimmy was a huge man, about 6'4", and loved to pick up my wife and swing her around. We had lunch with Johnny Rivers, Mike Massey (USA nine ball champ), and met one of my favorite entertainers ever, Jackie Wilson (Mr. Excitement) twice. So, to say the least, it's been a blast.

More important than any of the above are my three sons, their wives, and especially my grandchildren. I love them all dearly and always look forward to their visits.

We've had over twenty years of DJing experience to reflect on and many interesting people and events, mostly wedding receptions, that have kept me busy and young along with my associates who have been with me for many years. They are all a very important part of my life and have become my best friends.

Even through adversity, I feel the Lord has blessed us and given me a very full, enriched life and is still giving me daily lessons. And I love it!!

Mike Gintella
Mike's Light and Sound
BridesDJ.com

Don't Sabotage Your Own Wedding

Dave Petry
DJ Dave Productions

Are you looking to hire a DJ who is comfortable with you, easy to work with, and will give you one of the best nights of your life? You are in luck! My name is Dave Petry, and I am the owner of DJ Dave Productions, which is located in the greater Houston, Texas area. At our company, we strive to make your wedding reception the one you have been dreaming about your whole life. From our initial contact with you, we genuinely want to get to know you and your visions, desires, dreams, and goals. By knowing these things, we can work on a game plan that will help you have the wedding you've always wanted. Making all of these things happen isn't an easy task. It takes a lot of preparation and

planning.

I was born with musical DNA in my blood, and along with my wife of 36 years, Janet, who has premium event planning skills, we have been working together at DJ Dave Productions, rocking the dance floors for the last six years.

It all started when I wanted to be a musician. After following my dream and playing professionally in bands for a number of years, I finally discovered that the direction I really needed to go was in the DJ industry. I knew I could really build and grow a successful business. I had previous experience working in the corporate world, running national sales teams for companies, so I already had the understanding of the marketing side of things and how to intertwine that with growing a business. All of that experience came together, and DJ Dave Productions was formed. We first started off as a general DJ service, but now we have specifically decided to focus on the wedding market. This has been extremely successful for us. However, our true goal in our craft is to give you a special day—one that will create a lifetime memory for you and your spouse.

Lucky for you, creating one of the most memorable nights you will ever experience comes naturally to us. By getting to know you first, we can adequately prepare and plan for your special night. We like to know your favorite colors, hobbies, songs, your college alma maters, and things you like doing together. Based on that information, and with our exceptional music programming talent, we provide you with the most up-to-date trends and options available within the wedding industry. Also, we make sure that everything regarding planning the evening's entertainment is as easy as possible. This starts with our easily accessible and informative website, followed by a very good social media presence, and lastly, regularly updated videos so you can see the work that we have done. We also teach you how to better understand every aspect of planning your wedding—from the vendors, to decor, to finding the perfect venue.

For example, one of the more memorable weddings that we have recently done was a result of the whole educational process we walked a couple through. They took some of our ideas and thoughts and put together a movie-themed wedding because they had first met each other at a video rental store. The whole day had different acts. Act 1 was the wedding. Act 2 was the reception dinner. Act 3 was a grand entrance! Each of the tables at the reception had a movie genre theme, such as western, action, wedding, or musical films. This theme allowed us to have a big screen slide show on the front of the stage, as if you were at an actual movie theater! This design was great for our clients and company because we provide a lot more services than just music. We were able to help the couple with complete event coordinating, lighting and custom monogramming, slide show preparation, and, of course, the music played on the dance floor. No one will ever forget that wedding!

By giving us the necessary information and letting us do the work, you can have a memorable wedding, too. One of the first things that I always ask a couple is this: "In three words, how would you like your wedding and reception to be remembered?" That is the blueprint of how I get started. From there, the ball just keeps rolling until we have a magnificent night planned. I want to understand what your vision is and to be on the same page as you. What is most important to you? Is it the venue, food, entertainment? Or is it something else? Like I said before, the education process is very important at DJ Dave Productions. I will try to guide you and educate you as to how important the entertainment is and how much it will influence the success of the overall experience.

If you plan to spend $3,500 on a veggie tray and only $1,000 on entertainment, we can rearrange your budget in order to build the entertainment side to make it more memorable. After all, it isn't the veggie tray that your guest should be remembering most about your wedding! Most couples just need guidance when it comes to planning the wedding and reception. We at DJ Dave Productions act as consultants for you, not salespeople, and that is something that most couples really appreciate. We are very down to earth, and we don't push anything on anyone. All we want to do is find out what you want to accomplish and build your night from the ground up. Our main goal is to make sure that your wedding reflects your personality and style—that's what everyone will remember. Ultimately, we are here to help you and get you what's needed to satisfy your lifelong dream and make your wedding totally you.

On top of all of that, we are very reliable. Once you sign with us, we will be the DJs coordinating and performing at your wedding. There are some DJs who don't make this guarantee. In one instance, I received a call on a Friday at 3:30pm from the mother of a bride. She had just received a call from the DJ that her daughter originally signed with, and he was going to be a no-show. This was an elegant wedding with about 300 guests at one of the most prestigious venues in the Houston area. It just so happened that it was one of those rare Friday nights where I was actually free. I told her that I would DJ the wedding. I rushed over there and got set up an hour before the wedding was to begin. The groom graciously emailed me his playlist of all the special songs, and while I was driving over to the reception hall, I was downloading songs on the spot. Long story short, we pulled off the reception, and it went perfectly! The bride

and groom and their parents were so gracious and could not believe how well the night went on such short notice. Normally, preparing for a wedding takes a good 40 to 50 hours. This was done in a very short timeframe, and I attribute this to the fact that we have the experience and knowledge to make miracles happen.

Based on our experience, take this advice: when picking an entertainment service, take your time! Make sure you educate yourselves on how to select the best service available. This doesn't apply to just the entertainment service, but all your vendors as well. Start planning 12 to 18 months before your wedding date. The earlier you book your vendors and location, the sooner you pick your food and create a reasonable budget for your wedding, the better off you will be. The worst thing that can happen is to not give yourself enough time to call vendors and set up a location way in advance. Everyone will be booked, and you will end up getting the bottom-of-the ladder quality entertainment and providers.

So, to not get snubbed early on, it is very important to have a date picked out and find a venue. Then, obviously, entertainment should be third on the list. Afterwards, there is a multitude of things to plan, from your wedding dress all the way down to the caterer. We are often able to help our clients select other vendors through our recommendations. This makes us more valuable to the client because we aren't a company that will just play music for you—we will help you with other planning.

DJ Dave Productions definitely offers more than what an average company would offer. There are plenty of DJs who would be happy to accept your playlist and just play it. That is not quality entertainment, and it is something that you should not be paying for. We are here to guide you to have the most successful reception ever. There have been couples that we crossed paths with that merely gave us a playlist and told us what songs to play. This is a huge mistake when it comes to planning your reception! We understand that it is your wedding and your special day, but that does not necessarily mean that you have to make all of the decisions, either. Many couples can sabotage their wedding that way. You need to consider yourselves, but also consider your guests and what things they would enjoy. Try to engage them as much as possible. Think about what the guests want to hear in order to have a good night that they will remember for a long time. Be unique. Be different. But make sure to incorporate your guests' needs into that uniqueness when you are planning.

A great example of this is the tradition that some couples observe at their wedding in the greater Houston area. It is a German and Polish tradition where a grand march or entrance starts the reception. The guests put their hands up and make a tunnel for you and your new spouse to walk through. At the end of the grand march, the guests circle up around you afterwards. It is a really cool thing because it gets all of your guests involved, and it will be something that they can remember about the most important day of your life.

That is what we strive to do at DJ Dave Productions—make your wedding day the most important and most memorable day of your life. If you want a day like this, make sure you don't skimp on your entertainment. Ask questions when looking at different DJ services. How long have they been in business? Do they have back-up equipment? Are they insured? How many weddings do they do a year? Then, make sure to look at their reviews and testimonials from other people. This is huge for our company. We have grown so much over the last six years because of all the great referrals and testimonials from past clients. But, even as we grow, we don't want to lose our uniqueness as a company, willingness to help you plan, and ability to coordinate your wedding and reception, providing you with a great memory that will last a lifetime. So, for an all-around grand experience that will have you and your guests remembering your special day for years to come, take a look at DJ Dave Productions. You won't be sorry! We definitely look forward to meeting you soon!

About David Petry

Hello, my name is David Petry. Our company name is DJ Dave Productions, and we're located in Houston, Texas. We specialize in providing DJ and entertainment services for weddings and receptions. Last year, we performed our services for 55 weddings. We're a single operator; this keeps us very busy, and we currently have 80 weddings booked so far this year. Our business for the future looks fantastic!

I have been a musician and playing bass guitar since I was seven years old. I have played in several bands and recorded several different albums in the studio, with The Rafters, Behind the Scene, and Colourful Freedom. These albums are currently selling on iTunes. My love and passion for music led me down the path to become a professional DJ over six years ago. Since then, life has been fun and adventurous. My wife Janet is my partner, and together we make an incredible dynamic team for our clients. When you hire DJ

Dave Productions, you get both myself to act as DJ and Master of Ceremonies and provide entertainment and lighting services, then as a bonus, my wife helps to coordinate every little detail of every wedding and reception. We provide a very personalized, professional, hands-on service that is unique and customized especially for each individual client to make the special day fun, exciting, memorable, and reflect the individual personality and style of the client. We create unforgettable memories!

A Special Offer!

DJ Dave Production offers a FREE INSIDER SECRETS REPORT that has helped hundreds of brides and grooms plan their wedding. **Do you want your wedding to be unique and personal and not the same-old, run-of-the-mill, cookie-cutter wedding?** Please visit our website at www.djdaveproductions.com/freereport to sign-up for your free report **"37 Easy, Cheap (Or Free!) Ideas for a Wedding That Is Totally You."** **You will be glad you did!**

DJ Dave Productions
713–806–1085
info@djdaveproductions.com
www.djdaveproductions.com

Surviving Wedding Worst-Case Scenarios Like a Champ!

Mari Odette-Kanotz
A Amorè Events and Entertainment

Do you want to be part of a fun-filled, enjoyable, and successful reception? My name is Mari Odette-Kanotz, and I am the owner of A Amorè Events and Entertainment LLC, located in Issaquah, Washington, and serving all of the western Seattle, Washington, area. Getting to know you, your family, and your guests is one of my primary goals. By doing so, I can create an itinerary that is completely unique for everyone involved with your special day. Also, by getting to know your family, I can suggest "customs" that will make your reception fun and memorable! After getting to know your desires, I aim to take control of your crowd and create the ambiance you have always dreamed of. Bottom line, I do whatever it takes to make your reception as successful as possible.

At 4 feet 9 inches tall, I might be the smallest non-dwarf female DJ, but what I lack in height, I make up in my presence and personality. Over the last 18 years, A Amorè Events and Entertainment has been a premium DJ service that has helped thousands of couples make their wedding reception one of the most unforgettable events of their lives! Getting to the point of owning and operating one of the most successful DJ companies in the area didn't happen overnight. Before I was ever a DJ, I was a bride. I had attended many bridal shows to find vendors, and while I found many of them to be real professionals, the one industry that made me cringe was the DJ industry. When I dealt with DJs, I felt as if I was being attacked by used car salesmen. They all seemed to have one thing in common—more concern for their own ego than for another's events.

Because of my bad experiences with DJs, I passed on having one at my own wedding and decided I would do it myself. That's right—I was my own DJ! Since I had a background in theater and production, I thought I could pull it off. I was the one we refer to today as the "iPod bride"—but back then it was cassette tapes! Of course, being the bride and coordinating my own wedding created more stress than I needed on my actual wedding day. I had to make all of the announcements and corral all of the guests through the timeline. Although it was a nice wedding, it could have been more enjoyable for me if I had someone else to handle all the commotion.

After this experience, I realized that the person with the microphone should be the person guiding the entire flow of the event.

Events such as weddings are productions, so there needs to be a "production director" making sure that the end product looks the way it was originally envisioned by the bride and groom. With this philosophy in mind, A Amorè Events and Entertainment LLC, was formed, and we haven't looked back since.

I have to say, I love being with people and making their events special. I have an absolute passion for what I do. I am definitely not the type of DJ that just does it for the money, or simply enjoys playing music. I am genuinely concerned with how memories will be formed as each event is played out. I will hold your hand through the initial stages, the overwhelming planning process, and right up until the final song that is played at your reception. When we meet, my first question to you will be "What are the three words to describe your ambiance?" From there, a magnificent night will be created! Additionally, throughout the process, I will communicate with you about everything, and continuously verify that we are on the same page in regards to your wants and needs. I also want to make sure that I can provide as many services to you as I possibly can, and make sure that your special day is as successful as ever.

Having personally done over 2,000 weddings, I have a knack for keeping people happy and resolving problems quickly. An instance that comes to mind is when one couple was hosting their wedding in their backyard. Of course, being in Seattle, you always have to plan on rain, even in the summer. Luckily, I recommended tents for the outside event because, sure enough, it poured that evening! Overcoming the rain was a success, but, unfortunately, that was only our first hurdle. At one point, the caterers fell behind in meal service. Being attuned to every detail of the event, I saw the problem and offered a solution. To help them out, I started serving food, wine, and whatever else was needed. Additional guests arrived at the reception, and I set extra place settings and served them their food. Once dinner had concluded and it was dark out, the dancing began. However, the bar was put in a place with no lighting. Instead of putting undue stress on the bride and groom, I ran to my vehicle during a dance song, got extra lights, set them up near the bar, and the problem was solved. After the event, the couple let me know that the family video that was taken of their ceremony had terrible audio. Since I had taken footage throughout the evening, without a second thought, I sent them over mine. As you can imagine, the couple was extremely grateful at the end of it all.

"I love being with people and making their event special. I have an absolute passion for what I do."

Generally, good communication and knowing who you are and what you like as a couple can help quickly resolve many problems. However, sometimes the problems are consistent throughout the night. This person doesn't show up, or that vendor isn't listening to what you are saying. Complications like this can and often do happen. A good DJ should know how to solve problems on the spot.

There was another wedding I was doing back in 1997, and because of a 52-car pileup on I-5, all of the guests were late—even the minister. The bride was in the bathroom crying, and everything started off just horribly. After three hours, the missing guests started arriving, and the minister was able to marry the couple. After that experience, I became ordained, just in case, so that nothing like that would ever happen and I wouldn't have to deal with a crying bride with nothing to do about it. As you can tell, I despise not having solutions to problems! It's a good thing I took this step, too, because since becoming ordained, I have performed about 25 emergency ceremonies. So, when the officials don't show up or are late, I can actually officiate for them. Clients feel relieved knowing that no matter what happens, I can fix just about anything.

This is something that you should definitely be looking for in a DJ: someone willing to do almost anything and everything to make your day as perfect and special for you as possible. When you have hired your DJ, or any other vendor, for that matter, make sure to take full advantage of their experience, talent, and skills. For example, I incorporate event planning assistance into all of my packages at no extra cost. Not everyone takes advantage of this, but the people who do are so grateful. They notice that things went so much better than they imagined because of my added input. Also, make sure that your DJ gets to know you, really know you! The better that he or she knows you, the more comfortable your wedding is going to be, and the more fun you will have at your reception.

However, just because a DJ knows you well does not necessarily mean that he or she will only play songs that you like. Obviously, if you request us to play off a specific playlist, we will honor your decision. However, when relying on your playlist alone, we cannot guarantee that all of your guests will be dancing and having a good time. It is always nice if you give your DJ a little room to play around with songs, read the crowd, and create a fun atmosphere for all ages. If you like certain genres of music that may not go well at the reception, then try to incorporate them in the actual ceremony. That way, you can get what you want, and the guests can have a good time, too. If you do not allow the DJ to utilize his or her crowd-reading skills, your party might just be okay when it could have been spectacular!

Above all, the best advice that I can give you as a couple is to just relax, participate, and enjoy yourselves! It's your own wedding, after all, so let the people you hired handle the stress. Furthermore, invest the time to hire quality people so that they don't cause you any undue stress. Make sure that you have complete faith and trust in whoever you are hiring. If you need to micromanage the entire day, you obviously have not selected vendors that you think will do a good job. Invest the time to look at each vendor, consider all of the options, see what fits into your budget, and then make your decision. When you sign with A Amorè Events and Entertainment LLC, you will not only have a wonderful night, you will be walked through every single detail that makes up your special day.

Being located near Seattle, which is a port city, I have had the opportunity to witness many cultural customs from around the world. I actually have clients that sign with me and I never meet them until the actual event because they are across the Pacific Ocean. They do all of their booking by email, but because they live far away, they come here because it's an easier place for everyone around the world to fly into. Acknowledging cultural traditions is fun and should never be viewed as a burden by your DJ.

So, whether you're looking for a simple or extravagant wedding, we do it all! We will help you plan your special day so that it is an incredible memory you will never forget. With our event planning knowledge, passion for making your reception unique and successful, love for meeting new people, and extensive communication and follow-up on every detail, you don't have to worry about a thing when you sign with A Amorè Events and Entertainment LLC. We'll take care of you so you can have the time of your life! I certainly look forward to meeting with you soon.

About Mari Odette-Kanotz

Mari Odette-Kanotz has been entertaining since the age of two! She has performed as a professional actor, dancer, and singer in musicals, theatre, video, and motion pictures. She studied business and communications and was trained in theatre lighting, sound, and video production, as well as acting, jazz dance, ballet, tap, and voice.

Mari's interest in the wedding business began in the early eighties with her grandfather doing video production. She has since been involved in the limousine industry, catering, party planning, and event coordination.

Mari opened the first-of-its-kind, interactive children's play stage and was featured in a business publication as an "innovative woman-owned business operator." The facility offered services such as on-site parties, hands-on theatre, specialized instruction, junior nightclub, karaoke, retail costumes, and performing supplies.

In 1994, Mari began as a mobile disc jockey, and she quickly learned that this is where her talents could be most utilized to reach the largest audience. She became an ordained minister in 1997 after a freak accident had caused the officiant at one of her ceremonies to be three hours late. She decided to become ordained "just in case" she was needed in a pinch. She continues to perform many ceremonies on request—including a few that saved the day!

Mari has the natural ability to motivate a crowd and make them feel at ease. Her love of life and others shows in her smile and her work. Mari is the most requested female mobile disc jockey in the Pacific Northwest and frequently travels the West Coast and anywhere else she is requested to perform events.

Her skills as a true professional in an industry with a not-so-professional reputation are proven time and again through the referrals and compliments received from facilities, event planners, previous and current clients, and other wedding professionals.

A Amoré Events and Entertainment
888–942–6673
425–427–8964
www.seattledj.com
www.amore-events.com
www.facebook.com/AmoreEvents

To Plan, Anticipate, Celebrate, and Remember

Nick Javier
It's Time Entertainment

To plan, anticipate, celebrate, and remember...these are THE four main components that make up any of life's special occasions.

If you reflect back on the most memorable events of your life, they all contain these components. When you are lucky enough to find an individual who has made it his or her mission to weave these into the very fabric of a business, amazing experiences are the result. That core belief has driven Nick Javier for the past four decades. Since 2002, his company, It's Time Entertainment, has helped to create some of the area's most memorable weddings, corporate events, and custom private functions in and around

Sacramento, California, and the Northern California Bay Area. In recent years, Nick has also been called upon to perform events in Seattle, Salt Lake City, Scottsdale, Santa Cruz, San Francisco—and other cities that don't start with the letter "S" as well.

Where did it all begin? Back at Coronado High School in Scottsdale, Arizona, in the early seventies, Nick discovered that music was a positive distraction from being overly shy. From the time he purchased his first vinyl record (Chicago Transit Authority, a double LP), he knew there was something more to this medium than just album art and noise. The vast knowledge of contemporary jazz and rock artists and their music gave Nick (the teenager) the pathway to integrate himself into the many varied social groups that were prevalent in school. Gravitating towards the phonograph or 8-track player at the house parties was a way to contribute to the "party vibe" without calling attention to himself. Little did Nick realize that he was just auditioning for his own future!

HISTORICAL FOOTNOTE*:

* In 1971, the "dinner house / discotheque" concept was introduced to the Phoenix area by restaurateur Bob Sikora and a local radio DJ personality, Ray Ford, who updated and encapsulated the "dinner and dancing" experience under one roof...and voila!—Bobby McGee's Conglomeration was born! By 1974, this restaurant chain (now with five Southwest locations) would play an integral role in proliferating the international and national "disco" movement of the seventies, especially west of the Mississippi River. They would help change the way families, couples, and singles would experience nightly entertainment for the next two decades as they grew to over

18 locations, from Charlotte, North Carolina, to Honolulu, Hawaii. *

The Ice Bucket

Along comes Nick Javier, who, at 19, was trying to find his way in life after graduating high school in 1972 and community college in 1974. Answering an ad for employment, Nick was hired as a busboy at the original Bobby McGee's in Scottsdale, Arizona. It was a typical summer job, as he had already been accepted at Northern Arizona University in Flagstaff to continue his academics in the fall.

"This will keep him off the streets."

Little did he know, but that statement would hold true for the next 40 years!

Part of his duties as opening busboy was to periodically fill and take ice buckets from the kitchen, truck them across the dance floor, and deliver them to the bartenders in the lounge. As he was doing his duties one afternoon, he noticed that the dining room had a very cool radio station piped in. Music during setup—very nice! As the young employee emerged into the lounge area from the kitchen with the ice buckets, the radio broadcast was clearer and louder. As Nick's feet hit the wooden dance floor, he stopped—stunned—because it wasn't a radio station broadcast being piped in. In fact, there was a live disc jockey, in a booth—right there in front of him, The Golden Voice—spinning the vinyl, creating the very "show" Nick had been listening to for the past 20 minutes!

BAM!!!

"It was all over for me. I knew what I wanted to do for the rest of my life."

HISTORICAL FOOTNOTE**:

** And just recently (April 2012), I reconnected with Bob Williams, the DJ at Bobby McGee's who was setting up his nights' program that summer afternoon in 1974. He is currently the PA Announcer of the Colorado Rockies and Arizona Diamondbacks Spring Training facility in Surprise, Arizona. Thank you, Bob! **

During my first semester at NAU that fall of 1974, I was hired as head waiter at a restaurant similar in concept to Bobby McGee's (there were lots of imitators) called Granny's Closet. The owners allowed me to change records in the DJ booth between the lunch and dinner shifts, so I was ready when they offered me the lead DJ position in October. I embarked on my new career at the amazing wage of $2.75 / hour. Not bad for a 20-year-old on his own.

"I AM A DJ!"

The hunger to learn, coupled with a positive attitude, led me from Flagstaff, Arizona, to DJ in Fort Wayne, Indiana; Detroit, Michigan; Sacramento (in 1978); and then back with Bobby McGee's in 1980—this time as an established club DJ. That's when the real tour of duty started. I moved with them to Scottsdale, Phoenix, Dallas, Arlington, Houston, Denver, Newport Beach, and Long Beach until the early nineties.

Never mind the bell-bottoms, paisley shirts, and platform shoes

and line dances of the seventies. Never mind the fluorescent colors and flashy, Southern California lifestyle of the eighties and nineties. I would soon come to realize that those formative, traveling years would reveal to me important key concepts for my future as a Mobile DJ.

LEMONS INTO LEMONADE

1974—Mixing "Sing a Song" by Earth, Wind, and Fire INTO "I Love Music" by The O'Jays, and "Long Train Running" by the Doobies INTO "Heaven Must Be Missing An Angel" by Tavares—WITHOUT pitch control! Just Russco Studio Pro turntables with a 33/45 gear, and 500 lbs. of sand to deaden the rumble under each table. Oh... and the precise use of "thumb pressure" on the 45 to affect speed— without making it skip!

1974 to 1976—Using your voice as a tool, to segue between songs. Inflection, and the use to excite or relax an audience at any given moment...

1978—When my microphone went out on a Saturday night,

understanding and mastering how music programming alone can predict and steer the ebb and flow of a dance floor, as well as sell more liquor for the house...and a raise for me...

1980—Bobby McGee's DJ Training Class would teach me how to program dinner, early evening, transition, and late-night sets, utilizing the best music and artists from the big band era to the present day. This education would prove INVALUABLE as a Mobile DJ in the 21st century, as the age demographic and musical tastes of the client would not necessarily be the same, decade to decade.

1990s—As a corporate account manager in Freight, Wireless & Telecom, while still doing DJ events part-time, I developed the sales skills necessary to book and maintain high-level private and corporate clients. Those skills remain with me today, as I have maintained my DJ business on a full-time basis since 2008. Most of my business (90%) is from referrals, which I learned to cultivate back in the nineties!

1993—As I experienced my second (and last) marriage to my wife Joan, I realized how important a role a DJ plays in the flow of such an important event...mainly because we didn't have one! The importance of choosing the proper vendors to service your event cannot be understated. That knowledge constantly drives me to learn new and better ways to present my craft and skills, along with providing my clients with the very best reliable, quality equipment that the market may provide.

2001—While at Premier Entertainment in Sacramento, I

learned the difference between a DJ and an MC/DJ. Worlds apart. Ask Randy...he knows.

ITE—First Decade

It's Time Entertainment (ITE) came from a bold moment. I had been frustrated, doing most of the work on events, while the established mobile DJ companies I represented would take the majority of the profits. One morning in 2002, my wife Joan said to me:

"Honey, it's time you went out on your own."

"It's time...It's Time...It's Time Entertainment—perfect!"

The rest of my life became clear, created just over the next few days.

The Mission Statement. The Marketing Plan.

The Tagline (To Plan—Anticipate—Celebrate—Remember).

The Logo (Timeless Events = A Sundial; changed to a Banded Collar Tux in 2009).

The Focus (Relentlessly Serving Clients' Needs and Their Vision).

The Difference (MC. DJ. Event Facilitator.)

I can humbly and candidly say that I wake up excited every day. The possibilities with my entertainment company are unlimited. I have facilitated over a thousand weddings since the first one I was a groomsman and DJ in, during the summer of 1978; I have facilitated hundreds of corporate events, private parties, and school, church, and sports club functions, all over the country. I have been a game show host and an auctioneer, I facilitated a first birthday party and a ninetieth birthday party, and I have worked both Hawaiian luaus and Mexican fiestas.

There is only one common thread, woven throughout my entire career...

I do what I do, for you, my client. My customer. My friend. Your smile tells me I have accomplished my goal—not just for now, but for the next time as well. That's how I know I am right where I should be.

I have an event to prepare for now. It's Time!

It's Time Entertainment
916–240–6425
nick@itstimeentertainment.com
www.itstimeentertainment.com

Keeping You Out
of the Danger Zone

Robert and Stephanie Poff
Station Identification Entertainment

When it comes to hiring a DJ, where does one begin? Besides just being "professional," which should automatically be the bare minimum you require from your DJ, what other measuring stick can a bride and groom use when picking the vendor that is going to have the "biggest" impact on their once-in-a-lifetime day? Hiring a DJ is not like walking into your local big box store and choosing between several different Blu-ray players, of which, you will probably purchase several in your lifetime compared to hiring a wedding reception host, which you will probably only acquire once or twice in your lifetime. So what do you want your guests to say as they leave your reception? Do you want them

The grand entrance.

Newlywed game.

saying, "Wow, that DJ sure was professional," or, "Wow, that was the best wedding reception we have ever been to!" It can be quite stressful when you start to think, "I gotta get this right the first time; there are no do-overs, and I want to make sure that all the other monies, emotional energy, and time I have spent on my wedding aren't wasted if I choose a DJ who can't keep my guests engaged during my reception." You don't want to see all your hard work and dollar bills roll out the door, as guests leave not minutes but hours early, leaving you feeling as if this was a dinner-based event where guests left right after eating. So what tools can you use, as a bride and groom, to make sure you and your guests not only have a "professional" evening, but an evening everyone will be talking about for years to come? Well, we are here to help! Our names are Robert and Stephanie Poff, and we are the owners of Station Identification Entertainment, located in Anaheim, California.

We take great pride in making your wedding day the most amazing day of your life. We believe in something we like to call "reception perfection." How do we achieve this, you may ask? We have gone beyond the basics and have studied the wedding reception format as if we were scientists in search of answers. What we have discovered are what we like to call "danger zones." We figured out why they happen and how to fix them.

We know that having a wedding is like having a second job, so in order to make life as easy as possible during the wedding process, we have created an extensive online members' planning area on our website with online planners designed exclusively for our wedding clients. We have a detailed planner for just about every aspect of your wedding reception. There is a ceremony planner, reception planner, music request planner, wedding trivia planner, and

Fun in the photo booth.

First dance with up lights.

grand entrance biographies planner. We have planners that allow the father of the bride, the mother of the groom, and the bride and groom to put their thoughts together to create recorded messages. We have a hotline that you will be able to call to leave messages to each other. That message is then played right before your first dance. On our website, we also have samples of our activities and itineraries. If you're having trouble trying to pick songs, we have listings within categories for events such as the bouquet toss, garter toss, first dances, and much more. So, our site is basically like a one-stop shop where you can do all your planning.

Once all of that is completed, we will have a final planning meeting with you. We spend about two hours with you, going through your different planners and putting together your itinerary. This meeting is about a month away from your wedding. We find that this works out really well as opposed to meeting with you just a few days before the big event. With more time, you are mentally and emotionally present. You haven't gotten to the part where your excitement and/or nerves has started to take over yet. At our final meeting, we go over everything—dot all the I's, cross all the T's, and answer any questions so that we are all on the same page, and everyone knows exactly what to expect.

A few days after the final meeting, we type up the itinerary for your whole day, from the moment the guests arrive at the venue all the way to their departure. Before we finalize this, you get a copy to approve. Once approved, we shoot off a copy to your specific venue and any other professional vendors that you have booked. Furthermore, it is a good idea to do this a couple of weeks before the wedding, so that if there's something that we missed, you or your vendors will be able to catch it, and we can fix it before it's too late. This process that we have developed and perfected through the years is nearly fool proof, and it gives you a tremendous amount of peace and reassurance not only on your wedding day, but leading up to the big day.

When I, Robert, was 17 years old, I started DJing. I remember the exact date. It was back on October 31, 1985. I went to a party with a friend, and we asked the host of the party if I could plug in my stereo system and play some music. Surprisingly, he said yes, so we brought in the gear. Becoming a DJ was purely accidental. It wasn't until about 1993, when I bought out my partner, that I went full time. Although my entrance into the profession was accidental, everything I've done since then to establish the best DJ Company around has been very deliberate.

For over 10 years, we've grown our business through referrals alone. We've been very fortunate to be able to continually get referrals from our clients and many wonderful venues here in Southern California. My wife, Stephanie, began to integrate herself into the company in 1997. By 2000, she was on full time, DJing and learning about the wedding process.

When it comes to the sequence of events during the reception, there's no better person to organize that than your DJ. When it comes to the reception, all decisions, more or less, are entertainment related. Our job is to create an itinerary and a timeline that gives as much detail as possible to circumvent any major issues. We believe that the more detail we have, the less possibility there will be for any issues to arise. Being attentive to detail is what we pride ourselves on, and it sets us apart from other DJs.

We are also proactive. Whether it is an emotional fire or an actual one, we believe that every horrendous issue that could be encountered at a wedding reception should be and can be avoided.

Dinner ice breaker finale.

Station Identification staff.

It all goes back to our final planning meeting and simply preparing better. The online reception planner is key to this. At wedding receptions, we have identified issues that we refer to as danger zones. A danger zone is when the guests are starting to lose interest. It usually means that they are waiting for something to happen as the bride and groom are finishing something up.

For instance, danger zones can occur when the bride and groom do their table greetings. This is probably one of the most boring times at a wedding because, unfortunately, most wedding coordinators and DJs just stand around waiting for the bride and groom to finish their conversations. The bride and groom have to watch the clock. They have to monitor how long they're supposed to spend at each table. They're supposed to peel themselves away from the table they're at in order to talk to the next table, which can be an uncomfortable transition.

At Station Identification Entertainment, we have a couple of approaches to help brides and grooms in this awkward situation. One idea is to assign somebody as your table escort. This person's job is to watch the time and make sure you're spending only two or three minutes at each table. When it's time to go to the next table, they tactfully excuse you to move on. This is just one of many tips and helpful hints we share with our clients.

Also, we are known for icebreakers. Since danger zones exist when the bride and groom are finishing their last tables, when the guests are done eating, this is a perfect time to infuse some energy and fun into the party. We've developed some really cool dinner icebreakers that couples can choose from. In southern California, we're famous for our fun and creative icebreakers; you can check out some of them on our website. While you're online, if you go to weddingwire.com, yelp.com, or weddingchannel.com, you'll see that we've won the Best of the Knot Award for 2010, 2011, and 2012. What's cool about the award is it's based on actual reviews. Our reviewers share a common expression, "best wedding reception ever," and they continue to mention the renowned icebreakers.

Some people may think of icebreakers as the cheesy outdated follow-along dances, games, and routines that were very popular 10 or 15 years ago. Yes, times have changed, but instead of accommodating this change, some DJs just cut the fun altogether and do nothing. That left a really big void in the night, so we decided to create something that wasn't cheesy, something fun and competitive for the guests to do as a way for them to get to know one another. By doing this, we build relationships in an organic way that isn't forced like the old methods from years ago.

The DJ really only has three hours to build a relationship with your guests, so this is a perfect time to get things started. By building relationships with your guests early, when we do get to the dancing portion, the dancing will begin right away because people are no longer shy and are now feeling comfortable with their surrounding and the people around them. People don't necessarily dance because they love the music, they dance because they love the people they are with and are comfortable enough to let lose. Our icebreakers get them to that point! Too many DJs do nothing with guests and then expect them to engage in dances and routines just because they play certain songs. It's silly for a DJ to do no relationship building with your guests and expect them to comply with their instructions. We want to make sure that when your guests leave, they leave saying, "This was the best wedding reception I've ever been to."

This was the case at one reception at Old Range Country Club in Seal Beach, California. The entire day was just perfect! The ceremony was flawless, and because we provided lighting that created a really cool ambience by illuminating the ballroom, the reception looked gorgeous. The guests really enjoyed the photo booth out in the foyer that we set up, and of course, we did our famous icebreakers. This couple was so blown away that they took the time to write a letter for us to share with our prospective clients. Here it is:

To whoever is contemplating choosing Station Identification as their wedding DJ, simply put, Station Identification will be the best investment you will make for your wedding. This is not an exaggeration, an overstatement, or a sales pitch. To say that we were extremely happy with how perfect our wedding event was would be an understatement. Rob's expertise and passion for his craft made us so comfortable with our decision because we knew that we would have someone in our corner that wanted us to have the time of our lives, and we did.

I'm so happy that this couple could see and feel that we were there for them. Our livelihood depends on the success of your wedding. We don't advertise, so we literally live or die by how successful your event is. Our clients know that we care just as much about the success of their wedding as they do.

But, some things don't always go as planned. There was one instance at a reception where the father of the bride did a 30-minute toast, and it was not entertaining by any means. It meandered, was boring at times, and he just kept going on and on and on. Because of this, we had a shorter timeline to work with. I wasn't able to fix anything with the toasting because when you've got the guy who paid for the whole thing speaking to his baby girl, there's nothing you can really do! I do own some Oscar awards music that you can play to cue people to wrap things up, but I wouldn't do this without permission, as it's still kind of rude.

So, since we were short on time, I pleaded with the venue to allow us to play for an extra 15 to 20 minutes. They agreed, so we had that extra dancing time back, but it was still kind of a party killer. Now what I do to avoid this from ever happening again is to tell my bride and groom that each person doing a toast has to be told that there is a time limit. They must remind them of this time limit at least three times before the wedding day. On at least three separate occasions, I want you to remind anyone giving a toast that he or she only has two minutes. The first time they absorb it, the second time, they are like, "Oh, yeah, I remember you said that," and by the third time, they know that you're serious. We ask for more time than we need so that in the worst-case scenario, if we have three people doing toasts, there's going to be a 15-minute time span between all the toasters. We also don't allow you to have more than three people speak at one time because, again, it tends to be a party killer.

Keeping the toasts from going on too long and getting out of hand will, you guessed it, eliminate another danger zone. Another way to make your wedding successful is to hire a DJ that is reliable and that you can trust. Make sure to have a conversation about the insurance policy, budget, and emotional time and energy that need to be invested.

If you've got $25,000 put aside for your wedding day, because we are the glue that holds everything together, you want to make sure that you hire a DJ service that can pull it off. You cannot decorate your event into success. You can have the most beautiful, floor-length linens with overlays, and the most extravagant centerpieces, but people will still leave early if they are not entertained.

No amounts of flowers are going to motivate people to get up and dance. For every hour your guests leave early, there's a significant percentage of your money, time, and emotional investment rolling out the door. Hire more than just a "professional" DJ, you need someone who knows the wedding day ins and outs and leaves you and your guests with the "wow" factor! Don't just leave something up to chance or hire a company because it is cheap or because you overspent in other categories for your wedding. It is a mistake you will be sure to regret.

Station Identification Entertainment services come with a money-back guarantee. This is unheard of in the wedding industry. Our money-back guarantee adds peace of mind that we really stand by what we do. Because of this, we've created a business where two-thirds of our prospective clients have been referred to us solely based on our performances.

We want to be your solution so that your special night is exciting from the moment the guests arrive until they depart. We hope that we have informed you enough about our services to check us out! We look forward to talking with you soon and helping you plan your ultimate day!

About Robert and Stephanie Poff

Robert Poff co-created Station Identification Entertainment in 1985 and went on to become the sole owner in 1993. His wife Stephanie, now a co-owner, operator, and DJ, joined Robert in his pursuit and love of entertaining in 1997. They currently reside in Anaheim, California, with their daughter

Cameryn. They have made the wedding industry a lifetime career choice, and they continue to grow and educate themselves through seminars and wedding networking groups so they may continue to renew their passion and inspire others with their love of creating amazing entertainment unique to each individual bride and groom.

When they are not busy creating "reception perfection," they enjoy being a part of their extended family, the Lutheran Christian Church. They are committed to their daughter Cameryn and her passion for competitive swimming with the Anaheim Aquatics Association.

They are known throughout Southern California for their unique approach to weddings and have won many awards, including the Wedding Wire's Bride's Choice Award 2009 through 2012 and Best of the Knot in 2010, 2011, and 2012. You can check out their reviews right from the brides and grooms themselves at www. yelp.com, www.weddingwire.com, and www.weddingchannel.com.

They can also transform your ballroom, giving it that extra special and elegant touch, with their amazing Tri L.E.D. decor lighting and adding fun to any event with their ever-popular photo booths!

The first step to finding out more about their unique services is to:

1. Schedule an appointment to view a recent wedding performance on DVD [see the secrets that have made them so in demand]
2. Take a sneak peak at their famous online members' area of their website with many planners, song samples, and resources to make wedding planning a snap.
3. Check out their demo room where you can see their state-

of-the-art computerized DJ systems, elegant lighting choices, or jump into one of their popular photo booths and take it for a test drive!

For more information, call Station Identification Entertainment or fill out an event inquiry form on their website.

Station Identification Entertainment
800–850–3472
stephanie@stationidentification.com
www.stationidentification.com

What Matters Most—
Experience You Can Trust

Tim MacMillan
MacMillan Entertainment Group

*D*o you want to hire a DJ company with a stellar reputation that has been built up through decades and ultimately ensures that you have the best time of your life? You are reading the right chapter, my friends! My name is Tim MacMillan, and I am co-owner of MacMillan Entertainment Group. We are located in Southern Ontario and operate in Mississauga, Toronto, Durham Region, and Peterborough. We take great pride in the fact that we are a multi-DJ company with many professionals on staff.

Don't worry—just because we have an extensive staff of diverse DJs doesn't mean we just send you any random one that is available for your date and hope for the best. We make sure to hire the best of the best and match them specifically to your style and needs. All of our DJs have at least ten years of experience in the wedding industry. We take into account all of your needs and wants and what you expect to see in a DJ when determining your perfect fit. Establishing a large, well-respected DJ company didn't come without a lot of hard work. Our long history of success in the industry is based on sending the right DJ to the right event, without exception.

Music has always been a big part of my life. I was raised by two of the early pioneer DJs in Canada, my parents, Scott and Cher MacMillan, and together, we have kept this DJ company in business for over 40 years. Longevity is rare in this industry, but we have been able to accomplish this because we not only know what we are doing, but we believe in it as well. We understand how important our services are to each and every client and take this responsibility very seriously. We don't consider our events "gigs" to earn a quick buck. The events we do are once-in-a-lifetime experiences, and we are truly proud and honored to play a crucial role in the success of your celebration. We don't feel that it is our job to put on a show; rather, we aim to highlight and accentuate your love story. You will never see us trying to steal your spotlight. Since our company focuses on weddings, we understand it is only about you! We enjoy making the party happen, not being the party!

Another benefit of having multiple DJs on staff is that it is easy for us to have another DJ scheduled for backup just in case the original DJ cannot make it. Although this rarely happens, this assurance makes life a lot easier for us all. You are promised a DJ at your event no matter what happens, and we guarantee the quality service that represents who we are.

One busy Saturday night, we got a call from a distraught bride because her DJ, who did not have any other DJs on staff, had not shown up at her wedding. Normally, we don't take these calls because we devote 100% of our attention to our existing clients, but since all of our staff was in place and our backups were available, we were happy to help. It turns out she was referred to us originally, but had decided to take a deal for less money with the other DJ. She later confessed to us that the financial savings were not worth the stress she experienced that night.

To avoid situations like this, might I suggest that you always get a written confirmation from your DJ and that you meet him or her before your event. If they say they have backup for the wedding night, make sure to get a name and phone number of this DJ. Unfortunately, throwing around the term "backup" is very common practice, but few services actually have it in place. Don't compromise the success of your wedding because a DJ can't or won't make these types of arrangements! Over our 40 years at MacMillan Entertainment Group, we have continued to make this investment in our clients' peace of mind. Annually, we pay out several thousand dollars to ensure DJs will be available to help in the rare case of catastrophe. It's just too important of a night to leave to chance. This is part of our worry-free promise.

Sometimes, despite our best efforts, things do not go as planned. For example, one stormy night, the power went out at a wedding we were doing. Luckily, it was after dinner, so most of the important scheduled events had already happened. Since we are prepared for disaster, our backup staff had access to a professional-level, battery-powered sound system that lasts for at least five hours. Anticipating our clients' needs, we invest in these systems for wedding ceremonies where no power is available. We were able to put this equipment in place, and the bride, groom, and their guests partied and danced the night away by candlelight.

That entire situation may have ended differently had they hired a DJ company that wasn't willing to make investments to ensure nothing ruins the day. Not only is preparedness crucial, it is very important to hire a DJ you can trust to be reliable. For this reason, I would advise you against choosing a DJ based on price alone. Certainly, you should have a budget, but note that price differences reflect the quality of service and, ultimately, impact value. The adage "you pay for what you get" is true. However, although it is important to invest in quality services, your DJ should be willing to accommodate your budget and not rope you into paying for things you don't want or need.

It is important to note that the cost of your entertainment will most likely be a smaller part of the wedding's overall expenses. However, experience is the number-one thing you should look for in a DJ. A pre-programmed list of the "best" songs stored on an iPod will never replace a DJ who is skilled at reading the crowd. I have heard sad stories from couples who used substandard DJs who do not invest in themselves or their business. You can never get your special night back, so I suggest investing in the quality entertainment that your night deserves.

In addition to quality, it is important that you make sure to plan and confirm all the details well in advance with all of your vendors. The more communication that occurs ahead of time, the better. Ultimately, if you hired a quality DJ, you need to trust that person. Providing a huge list of must-play songs ties the DJ's hands and prevents them from doing what they do best: getting the crowd excited and up and moving. DJs certainly appreciate guidance, but if you really want to have a great party, allow them to read the crowd, play requests, and make sure your guests have a great time.

I also suggest that you do not have your wedding planner arrange the musical aspects of your reception. Consulting with them about general-event planning is great because their expertise is in seeing the big picture. However, they are not experts in regards to the nuances concerning what music to play or what keeps people on the dance floor. By letting the DJ do what he or she does best, you can sit back and enjoy yourselves. Remember, you set the tone of your event, so it is important that you don't feel stressed because of logistical details. If you are on the dance floor enjoying yourself, the guests will be as well. So get up there and have fun!

These are just some quick and easy tips to consider when planning your reception, hiring vendors, and picking out your entertainment service. At the end of the day, you want to make sure that you are completely confident with every person you have hired. Consider these people your dream team, as they are responsible for turning your dream into a reality. I ask you to take a look at what MacMillan Entertainment Group has to offer.

Specializing in the wedding industry for over 40 years, we have an established reputation of trust and professionalism. Our distinctly stylized, experienced, high-quality DJs will be matched perfectly with you based upon your needs, wants, and interests. Our one-of-a-kind services will have everyone talking about your reception! Check us out, I'm sure you will find that MacMillan Entertainment Group is the right choice for you. MacMillan Entertainment Group —Experience You Can Trust!

About Tim MacMillan

Tim MacMillan operates the leading DJ entertainment company, MacMillan Entertainment Group, which has offices in three cities in Southern Ontario, Canada. Tim oversees the day-to-day operations of this over 40-year-old company that offers its clients more than 30 DJ entertainers to choose from.

MacMillan Entertainment Group is a family-owned company that also has a commercial music and pro audio and lighting division, Multi Music Group Inc. Tim has been involved in the DJ industry all of his life and has been actively spinning for over 20 years. He is the eldest son of industry pioneers Scott and Cher MacMillan, who, as the original founders of the parent company, are still very much involved today. MacMillan Entertainment Group is known industry wide to have the "experience you can trust."

Want more info? Contact us today by phone or on our website using the promo code BOOKDEAL for a special package just for you!

MacMillan Entertainment Group
905–615–8585
800–207–7747
Peterborough Office: 705–652–3421
Durham Office: 905–809–8616
djreservations@macmillangroup.com
www.macmillangroup.com

How Do You Know if You Hired a Great DJ?

Austin Giles
Outright Entertainment

Are you looking to have your guests dancing non-stop at your reception? Stop looking and start reading! My name is Austin Giles, and I am the owner of Outright Entertainment, Inc., located in Calgary, Alberta, Canada. What does it take to achieve the great dance party you've been searching for? Non-stop music for your reception that everyone can dance to! Everything from oldies and classic rock to today's top-forty hits and even culture-specific music—everything should be mixed live, specifically for you and your guests.

After DJing at the only roller rink in Calgary 10 years ago, I realized that I could take my talents to new heights. I started DJing at various nightclubs around Calgary, and I quickly learned that DJing requires a few key abilities. One key ability is being able to read a crowd. The DJ must adjust music as necessary based on crowd response. A DJ must also be able to mix music to where it is still danceable. With my experience and interest in the DJ industry, I started researching to see what it would take to start up a mobile DJ business and found that, although there was a lot of competition in the Calgary area, there weren't many businesses offering the level of service I felt was needed.

Soon after my research, I created Outright Entertainment, Inc., and we have been going strong ever since 2009. From weddings to corporate and private events, we do it all! At Outright Entertainment, the energy of our events is non-stop, with great tracks that keep the guests dancing right up to the last song. We achieve this by performing proper mixing techniques. For instance, in the nightclub industry, it is vital that a DJ is continually playing music and mixing songs together—a smooth transition from one song to the next by matching beats together. Surprisingly, however, this is not something that is really expected out of mobile DJs, and that is what sets us apart from many other mobile DJ businesses: We mix the music properly to ensure a danceable flow is maintained.

Mixing is very important to an event. In the Calgary area, there are many mobile DJs who play one song and then simply push "play" again on the next song once the last song has finished. By doing this, the DJ is disregarding one of the most important aspects of the job—to ensure that the music is *flowing* properly. When you think about it, what is the difference between an iPod and a DJ who does not properly mix the music? Not much. There is no flow to the music. With a properly trained DJ, you'll get music that flows smoothly from one song to the next without overdoing it by adding sound effects, scratching, or anything like that. It's the DJ's ability to read a crowd and keep a good music flow that keeps your crowd moving all night!

One of my focuses with Outright Entertainment, Inc. is to offer a DJ who has the ability to adapt his or her style to yours. It is common for many DJs to only play a certain set of songs and not change up the playlist for different events. What some DJs play at a club is exactly what they will play at a wedding. This is something that should not happen—especially at your wedding! Our DJs strive to listen to you and play what you want to hear. We are constantly changing our playlists to fit the essence of our clients. Your wedding should be one of a kind. It should be different from anyone else's. We ensure this by having you meet with the DJ performing your wedding beforehand to discuss, plan, and sample music preferences for your reception. Do not rely on a DJ's predetermined playlist to do the talking for you.

Reliability of the DJ is another very important factor to remember when considering DJ services. One experience that proved this to be true was when I was still DJing at a downtown nightclub. A DJ that worked with me at the club was supposed to provide wedding services for his friend, but he called me two hours before the ceremony started and said that he couldn't make it. I got the couple's phone number and met the bride outside of the reception hall an hour before the wedding started. She gave me a quick rundown of what she wanted—the music she wanted for the ceremony and for the reception—and I quickly adapted my style to her preferences. The ceremony and reception went off without a hitch, and it was a great party and an absolute blast! In that case, we were lucky that

I was able to provide services for her wedding at the last minute. Be sure that you feel confident in the DJ and company you book. It's important you feel that they are reliable enough for your special day.

Another interesting last-minute opportunity presented itself in Outright's first year of operation. I was scheduled to provide music for the closing ceremony of the 2009 WorldSkills Competition, which is similar to the Olympics for people in the trade industry. This event is held at a different city around the world every four years. The closing ceremony was held in a stadium with about 8,000 guests, and just as the show was about to begin, there was a problem that needed 20 to 30 minutes to fix. The directing manager asked me if I could DJ for the crowd and the participants while they fixed the problem.

I accepted the opportunity, of course. After I transitioned into the second song, some of the competitors grabbed their country's flags and started marching and dancing around the stage. Soon, nearly all of the participants and the crowd joined in and were loving the non-stop music. I got a lot of great feedback from that experience. The owner of the production company that was putting on the competition wrote me a letter that said, "The closing ceremonies, particularly the music, were so successful that the organizers of the next WordSkills in London admitted that they will be hard pressed to surpass the Calgary experience." At this event, I needed to read a crowd of 8,000 guests and make it memorable. It was a lot of fun, and I really enjoyed the experience. You'll know that you've hired a great DJ if he or she has the ability to adjust his or her entertainment style to suit a diverse crowd of any size.

How else do you know that you have hired a great DJ for your most special day? Asking questions is extremely important. I'm not talking about "What kind of music will you play?" kind of questions. Ask more serious questions to determine whether your potential DJ is legitimate and well suited for you or not.

Good Questions to Ask a Potential DJ:

- Is the company insured?
- Do you have past references from wedding couples? (Ideally from the most recent wedding season.)
- What are your rates for weddings and what could cause the rate to increase? (Hourly or set price?)

A mobile DJ needs to be insured. Insurance is important so that if something happens to the DJ, one of the guests, the equipment, or the venue, the costs would be covered. Most likely, nothing of that nature would happen at your reception, but, as the adage goes, "it's better to be safe than sorry." In addition to insurance, having past references to look at or talk to is key. Written reviews are great, but if you ask, the DJ should also be able to put you in contact with recent clients so that you can ask them any questions you want. Talking with recent clients will help you learn more about your potential DJ and how he or she typically runs a wedding reception. Good reviews are obviously more likely to result in a good DJ and vice versa.

Finally, knowing your DJ's rate is important, but not for the reason that probably first comes to mind. Do not ask the DJ's cost so that you can compare pricing to find the cheapest DJ service. Ask so that you can be sure that you have set enough money aside for the DJ that you want! Not budgeting properly is the biggest mistake that I have seen couples make when planning their wedding reception. I would highly encourage you to set up a budget for your wedding just as you would with your monthly and yearly expenses in life. Obviously, you want a perfect life and a perfect wedding, but you need to be realistic and assign more money to the areas you believe will have a greater impact on your wedding day.

I realize that every wedding vendor can justify how his or her products or services could make your wedding day better, but I do feel the need to point out the importance of entertainment at your wedding. Time and time again, I hear from newlyweds that the venue and entertainment were the two most memorable things from their wedding reception (in terms of planning). Think about that for a moment. What do you honestly think you and your guests will remember more about your wedding day—the style of chair covers at the dining tables, for example, or whether they had a great dance party/celebration that night? With that in mind, I truly believe that you will have a better return on investment by allocating a few hundred dollars more towards something that will have a bigger impact on you and your guests' overall wedding experience.

So, once you have the DJ that you've budgeted for and are confident with, don't be afraid to try something out of the ordinary! You don't necessarily have to include everything that is done at a typical wedding reception, and you shouldn't be afraid to include anything that you feel might be fun or important—whether it is traditional or not. For example, at one wedding I provided entertainment for, the groom had actually chosen a female supermodel as his "best man"! Not only did this nontraditional decision work great, but it also became an ongoing discussion throughout the evening. How exciting and interesting would it be to have a supermodel as the best man?!

But please don't go out to find a supermodel friend if you don't have one. Doing your own thing can be as simple as adding a special song or announcement for your parents to dance together to, or it could, in fact, mean following the traditional reception format if you feel it suits you well. Just don't hesitate to include personal touches that are important to you. After all, it is your wedding, and the evening should reflect you as individuals and as a couple. Don't be afraid to think outside the box.

Some great ideas that I have seen at receptions include incorporating simple games throughout the evening. For example, instead of having your guests clink on their glasses to make you two kiss, you could have the guests tell a funny story about you two (the bride and groom), sing a love song, or even kiss their own partner in order to get you two to kiss! Preparing a fun choreographed dance for the bridal party entrance, first dance, or other dance to present to your guests is also a fun and exciting way to increase the excitement for the rest of the night.

If you know someone who is comfortable with public speaking, it is a great idea to have someone that you know as the emcee for the dinner and toast portion of your reception–like a close friend or relative. Although the DJ knows how to get everyone moving and makes a great emcee for the special dances and dance portion of the evening, the DJ isn't able to include personal history and humor that only your friends and family can appreciate. Having an emcee for the dinner and toasts who knows you and your family well will make the guests feel a little more relaxed and set the stage for a great time.

We realize that every wedding and couple is different, and that not all of these suggestions will work for everyone, but make sure to at least take these suggestions into consideration when planning your wedding reception. Trust me, you won't regret it! I hope these points have helped you understand a little more about the type of service that we at Outright Entertainment, Inc. provide. Please don't hesitate to contact us to discuss how we can help to make your personal wedding a great success. With our experience, adaptability, and reliability, we would love to work with you towards one of the most memorable nights of your life!

About Austin Giles

With more than 15 years of experience in the entertainment business—including experience as a nightclub, roller-rink, and mobile DJ—Austin Giles has combined his background in music, management, and performing arts to become an industry leader.

Since 2009, his company, Outright Entertainment Inc., has provided DJ and entertainment services for hundreds of successful weddings and many large-scale events in the Calgary area, including the closing ceremonies of WorldSkills Calgary 2009 with an audience of 8,000 (see it on YouTube at http://youtu.be/ch-9cI2soUs). His corporate clients include Enterprise Rent-A-Car, McDonalds, the Calgary Stampede, the Calgary Flames, WestJet, H&R Block, Enform, and Shell Canada.

As a member of the Young Canadians School of Performing

Arts, Austin spent eight years training and performing for international audiences of up to 20,000 in the nightly Grandstand Show at the Calgary Stampede—the "Greatest Outdoor Show on Earth." He has a bachelor's degree in communications and culture, and a certificate in professional management—both from the University of Calgary.

For more information, contact Outright Entertainment Inc.

Outright Entertainment Inc
587–333–4803
service@outrightentertainment.com
www.outrightentertainment.com

Making Your Reception a Memory, Not Just an Event!

Gerald Chmilar
Prairie Mobile Music

Are you interested in a DJ company that lets you call the shots, makes your dreams come true, and helps you along with the planning process leading up to your special day? You have just found your source of entertainment for your wedding! My name is Gerald Chmilar, and I am the owner of Prairie Mobile Music, located in Grand Prairie, Alberta, Canada. Our company strives to create an unforgettable atmosphere for your wedding reception. Whether it's up lighting, fog, snow, bubble machines, or the actual music, you can expect tremendous work and planning, followed by an unmatched performance from one of our professional DJs. We offer five different wedding packages for you to choose

Sandman Inn, Grande Prairie, Alberta.

Sandman Inn, Grande Prairie, Alberta.

from so you can make your night perfect and within your budget.

Additionally, we have great customer service. We believe the customer is always right. We go with the flow and do whatever you ask us to do. When it is all said and done, we want you and your guests to be happy and have an enjoyable evening. We not only create music, we create atmosphere.

It all started back when I was 14 years old. My dad had just passed away, and I bought my first cassette player. Living on a farm at the time, I did not grow up with much music. But after my father passed, I decided to see what it was all about. It quickly went from one cassette to 500 to 5,000, and I soon realized that music was something I really enjoyed.

At first, I became an accountant. I did that for nine years until one day I left to establish a full-time, multi-operational DJ business. That was in 1985. Now, in 2012, we are bigger and better than ever, making a difference in couples' lives all over Alberta.

Even though we are a bigger DJ company, our many DJs have one thing in common: passion! I do what I do because I have a passion to do it. I don't work for the money; I DJ because I love it. When I do it, I always have a genuinely good time providing entertainment. This passion is what allows soon-to-be brides and grooms anticipate the feel, the smell, the sound, and the look of their wedding day in real time. Even though it may be months away, it is a wonderful time to dream and to believe that anything is possible. During this time, it is important for the bride and groom to seek out that shared enthusiasm and, with the help of entertainment providers, to bring it all to life. These are the key attributes I look for when hiring other DJs. I also look for someone who is good at public speaking, good with people, and good with music. Professionalism and

Grande Prairie Inn, Grand Prairie, Alberta.

passion are what you can expect from your personal DJ at Prairie Mobile Music.

We consider many factors when planning your event. For example, older ears can be sensitive to louder music. With this in mind, our DJs will sit down with you to design a floor plan to decide where the DJ table should be and where the guests' tables will be. Also, if the Best Man or Maid of Honor doesn't like giving speeches, that's all right! Our DJs will work with you to provide the necessary tools and helpful hints to create a great, memorable speech. Finally, our DJs will "read" your crowd and play songs that will keep most people on the dance floor all night long. After all, music makes or breaks a party. Our DJs are trained to exceed your expectations and make your party memorable to you and your guests.

Although our DJ's are hired by me, they are ultimately working for you. You're the boss! They will bend over backwards for you to make sure that your night goes as smoothly as possible. For example, there was one occasion when the emcee at one wedding (not one of our master of ceremonies) was nervous because of the large number of people that were at the reception. Trying to calm her, someone offered her a drink. One drink turned into two, which turned into three, and so on. She ended up passing out before the introductions, and one of our DJs took over, threw some jokes together, and adjusted to the style of the bride and groom. Needless to say, the wedding was a great success!

Professional DJs are versatile and ready to go into any situation. Even though my DJ was not scheduled to be the master of ceremonies, he ended up making it a great night for the bride, groom, and their guests. It is important to focus on the customer in these disastrous situations. We will do exactly what you want—so tell us,

Crystal Center, Grande Prairie, Alberta.

and we will do our very best to accommodate you in whatever way possible.

Not all DJ companies will focus on you when something like this happens. A DJ may be too busy making him or herself look good, so they don't even ask for your input. For this reason, it is very important to not under-budget for entertainment for your wedding reception. There have been plenty of times that couples spent more on flowers and party favors than on their entertainment. Trust me, your guests will not remember the flowers and gifts they receive. They will remember their experience. Having a quality DJ directly correlates to your guests' perception of your event, so you cannot skimp on booking a DJ who will make your dreams a reality.

It is definitely worth planning a budget for all of the vendors you will hire. Make sure that you have an idea of how high you are willing to go in each of the major categories. This will help you narrow down your vendors, and you will know exactly how to negotiate what you are getting. Planning your budget is only some of the work, however. It is also vital that you plan your ceremony and reception accordingly. Make sure that everyone is on the same page by handing out basic timelines. The biggest mistake you can make is not planning enough ahead of time for the events of the evening. You want your wedding and reception to go smoothly, so plan it that way! Make sure to inform everyone of their duties and that everyone knows where to be and when. By doing so, there will be one less thing you will have to worry about on your special day.

Of course, worry is something that every couple faces when planning their wedding. Will your guests enjoy themselves? Will you and your mate enjoy yourselves? To eliminate some of this worry, incorporate things that reflect your personality as individuals

Center 2000, Grande Prairie, Alberta.

and as a couple into your reception. Try to wrap your mind around the elements that make your personalities magnetic. What attracts you to the people that you have just met, the ones you haven't, and the ones you want to meet? Let the things you love rule your reception—to a certain extent, of course.

Don't let the things you love completely overload your reception. This is a huge mistake that I have seen couples make. Don't pack too many speeches, slide shows, photograph presentations, and games into your reception, even if you love all of these things!

263

Stonebridge Hotel, Grande Prairie, Alberta.

Guests will lose interest if they see something more than once or twice. Limit yourself to no more than one or two presentations and spread them out throughout the night. Have no more than six short speeches (both sets of parents, Maid of Honor, and Best Man) during the night.

It is very appropriate and memorable to have some traditions or cultural activities as part of your reception. For example, in our area, there are a lot of French weddings, and there is a very cool tradition some French families observe. If the younger son gets married before the older son, the family gets a big metal tub full of ice and water, and the older son has to dance into it. Once he has one leg in and one out, all the ladies start to dance around him and mock him because his younger brother got married first. It is a really fun tradition, and our DJ's enhance it by playing some ridiculous fiddle music or something like that. The whole experience makes everyone laugh!

All in all, Prairie Mobile Music is a great company, with a lot of options for you to choose from, to make your day unforgettable. With state-of-the-art lighting, sound, and professional DJ skills, you will not regret signing with us. But don't just take my word for it. Make sure you check out our company website and see all of the referrals and testimonials of previous clients. Word of mouth has played a huge role in the expansion of our company, and we continue to strive to give our clients what they want and how they want it. I highly recommend considering Prairie Mobile Music for your wedding day. You and your guests will remember your night forever.

About Gerald S. Chmilar

Gerald S. Chmilar was born Easter Day in 1961, in Mundare, Alberta, Canada. He has three other brothers, and their parents owned a cattle and grain farming operation. Upon graduating from high school, Gerald earned a business degree through a correspondence university. Gerald then moved to Grande Prairie, Alberta, Canada in 1981 to pursue his accounting career. He bought his first disc jockey system in 1985, founding "Prairie Mobile Music." The following year, he purchased three more DJ systems, and in 1990, another seven DJ systems. Shortly after, he decided to leave his accounting occupation to pursue his DJ business. At this time, he was married with two sons.

By 1992, Gerald was running up to 15 DJ systems with various sizes of light shows and all kinds of special effects. In 2001, Gerald invested in big screen video productions, which allowed Prairie Mobile Music to expand its services to cater to larger audiences. He was then able to cater to video dance parties, extravagant weddings, and larger corporate functions. This was the start of Prairie Mobile Music's Elite and Ultimate Dream Wedding Packages.

> "We are the greatest DJ service in the Peace Country, covering a vast area. We are constantly outdoing ourselves by purchasing new equipment and trying great, new, fun ideas with our wedding couples. Every wedding I DJ gives me great satisfaction, especially the second-generation weddings; first we performed the parents' wedding, and then years later, their children's wedding."
>
> —Gerald S. Chmilar

Gerald's eldest son Jaden (also known by the alias DJ JayFresh) grew up in the music industry. He became one of the premier party rockers and pioneers of the Grande Prairie–area music scene. He has earned his spot to open and play along some of the biggest names around. Owner and founder of Funkin Your Area Productions, JayFresh has been one of the main promoters to bring major acts from all around the world.

Gerald's youngest son Dalen also has a paw in the music industry. He won elections two years in a row as VP Social of the Students' Association of Grand Prairie Regional College and has programmed and marketed the most successful events in Howlers' (student lounge) history. With major empowerment in his position, he was able to produce very unique atmospheres in his events for Grande Prairie's college and surrounding community.

Ever since Gerald started his disc jockey business, he always had a goal in leaving a legacy mark in the music industry. After pondering on this idea for many years, in 2006 Gerald got involved in manufacturing a very high-end audio-speaker system. This was the start of Particle Audio. It was a very long and hard road to pursue, involving not only the building of all the prototype speakers but also the patent protection process. Northern Alberta experiences extreme weather conditions that require this speaker to work in extreme cold temperatures and even outside in the rain with the grills off. This speaker has a high level of sound quality as well as having a minimal amount of ear fatigue for the listening audience.

If you are looking to book a disc jockey for your wedding or if you would like to purchase a set of speakers in the color of your choice, contact Prairie Mobile Music.

Prairie Mobile Music
780–538–1565
gerald@prairiemobilemusic.ca
www.prairiemobilemusic.ca

Final Words and Advice

Mark Imperial

Well, there you have it. Now it's up to you. I hope you enjoyed the book, and I'm sure you learned a few things. The choices you have to make your day memorable and stress-free are pretty obvious. My advice — hire a professional DJ Entertainer. It may be the best decision you make about your wedding.

If you're lucky enough to have one of the 18 co-authors of this book near your wedding location, your decision is pretty clear. You want to call them and set up a time to meet. They will most certainly take care of you.

If one of these top-notch professionals are not near you, then you have a little homework, but, don't worry, you are equipped. You know what to expect, and you know what to look for. Just follow the advice in this book, and you are on your way to a great day.

If you found this book useful, I encourage you to pay it forward and hand it to a friend or family member that is next in line to get married. When you hear about someone getting engaged, you can give them a great gift by handing them this book. The future bride and groom will thank you.

I, and the fellow authors of *The Ultimate Wedding Reception,* wish you great happiness on your upcoming wedding. May your plans be fruitful and your memories sweet. We wish you years of joy as you venture into a new life together.

Congratulations!